FRONTIERS OF FAMILY LAW

Frontiers of Family Law

Edited by

GARETH MILLER
Centre for Family Law and Family Policy
The Norwich Law School
University of East Anglia

ASHGATE

Published by
Ashgate Publishing Limited
Gower House
Croft Road
Aldershot
Hants GU11 3HR
England

Ashgate Publishing Company
Suite 420
101 Cherry Street
Burlington, VT 05401-4405
USA

Ashgate website: http://www.ashgate.com

British Library Cataloguing in Publication Data
Frontiers of family law.
  1.Domestic relations - England 2.Domestic relations - Wales
  3.Domestic relations
  I.Miller, J.G. (John Gareth)
  346.4'2015

Library of Congress Cataloging-in-Publication Data
Frontiers of family law / edited by Gareth Miller.
  p. cm.
  Includes bibliographical references and index.
  ISBN 0-7546-2274-6
  1.Domestic relations--Congresses. I. Miller, J. Gareth.

  K670.A6F76 2003
  346.01'5--dc22

2003057860

ISBN 0 7546 2274 6

Printed and bound by Athenaeum Press, Ltd.,
Gateshead, Tyne & Wear.

Contents

List of Contributors

Caroline Ball is a Reader in Law at the Norwich Law School, University of East Anglia.

Alastair Bissett-Johnson is Professor of Law at the University of Dundee. He was formerly Professor of Law at the University of Dalhousie, Halifax, Nova Scotia, Canada and has held posts at universities in England, Australia and Canada.

Brigitte Clark is a Lecturer in the Norwich Law School, University of East Anglia. She was formerly in the Department of Law at The Rhodes University, Grahamstown, South Africa.

William Duncan is Deputy Secretary General at the Hague Conference on Private International Law. He was a member of the Irish Law Reform Commission and Professor of Law at the University of Dublin.

Gareth Miller is Professor Emeritus at the Norwich Law School, University of East Anglia.

His Honour Judge David Pearl is President of the Care Standards Tribunal and also continues to sit as a Circuit Judge. He is a Bencher of Gray's Inn and was formerly Professor of Law at the Norwich Law School. He is an Honorary Professor of the University of East Anglia.

Liz Trinder is a Senior Lecturer in the School of Social Work at the University of East Anglia.

Prue Vines is an Associate Professor in the Faculty of Law at the University of New South Wales, Sydney.

Introduction

This is the third collection of papers published under the title 'Frontiers of Family Law'.[1] The series grew out of seminars given at the Centre for Family Law and Policy at the University of East Anglia, but also includes other contributions. The aim is to explore issues lying at the various frontiers of the subject we have become used to call 'Family Law'.

In Chapter 1 Caroline Ball looks at the drawn out process of reform of adoption law culminating in the Adoption and Children Act 2002. Other areas of child law received intense scrutiny in the decade leading up to the Children Act 1989. It has taken more than a decade to achieve the reform of adoption law that was recognised as necessary to meet the changed nature of adoption practice. The Adoption Act 1976 underpins the 'gift/donation' model on which adoption practice had been predicated since the legalisation of adoption in 1926. The changed nature of adoption practice and in particular the adoption of older children from care, required recognition of the so-called 'contract/service' model in which adoption is not the end of the process but a step in the process of family development which will continue to require support. She concludes that the blunt instrument of legislation is unlikely to provide all the answers in an area that remains one of deep complexity and sensitivity. Nevertheless, it is clear that the Adoption and Children Act of 2002 represents a very significant event in bringing the law relating to adoption more in line with the changed nature of adoption.

The two following chapters are concerned with access/contact between children and parents and explore problems associated with two different frontiers.

Liz Trinder is concerned with the boundary between law and private ordering in this difficult area which can give rise to great bitterness. She explores the relationship between two significant trends in family law. The first is the move to the promotion of private ordering to settle family disputes with the implication that parents rather than courts are the best people to decide post-divorce arrangements for children and consequently the active involvement of the courts or judicial determination should be restricted to those cases where parents cannot agree. The second major trend is the emergence of a strong although rebuttable legal presumption in favour of contact between children and non-resident parents after divorce. Both are subject to criticism. The private ordering principles and contact presumption are therefore contested and there are also indications that family practices are not wholly congruent with the intentions of legislators.

---

[1]   The first collection under this title, edited by Andrew Bainham and David Pearl, was published in 1993 and this was republished with the second collection edited by David Pearl and Ros Pickford in 1995.

The chapter explores what the law and the legal system does have to offer families making contact arrangements. Drawing on a recently completed study of contact decision-making Liz Trinder examines two questions. First: How pertinent is the law and the legal system in the making of contact arrangements? Secondly: What are the consequences of engagement and non-engagement with the law in making contact?

The role of law, in many cases, is minimal, even non-existent, with many families operating contact arrangements out of reception range of the shadow of the law but underpinned by common child welfare principles. This level of private ordering was in fact precisely what the architects of the Children Act 1989 had wished to encourage as much as possible. The research shows that a large group of parents take advantage of the Children Act 1989 to establish their own contact arrangements, while a significant group of parents either drop out of contact or experience conflict over roles or safety.

In general it seems that the no order principle and privatisation thrust of the Act has worked surprisingly well. However, when contact arrangements are not working the capacity of the law to mend them is inherently limited. Indeed in high conflict cases the law can be destructive rather than constructive, and expensive in emotional and financial terms for the participants. Nevertheless, the law does have things to offer children and parents who face difficulties in organising contact, and the chapter concludes by considering the contribution law can make in this often highly charged area.

William Duncan is concerned with problems of access/contact arising from physical boundaries. Contact/access problems are often difficult to resolve even where both parents are within one State. The problems are multiplied at the international level by the geographic distance, as well as legal, linguistic and other cultural differences between the countries concerned. William Duncan identifies the problems and in particular the relationship between such problems and the problem of abduction. He then sets out some fundamental principles relating to the right of the child to maintain personal relationships even when the parents live in different States, that appear in various international instruments. He goes on to identify and survey the different elements which impact on the resolution of international access/contact problems. The international picture with regard to jurisdiction to make or modify contact orders has up to now been a rather unsatisfactory one. It was against this background that negotiations began at The Hague for the Convention of 19 October 1996 on *Jurisdiction, Applicable Law, Recognition, Enforcement and Co-operation in respect of Parental Responsibility and Measures for the Protection of Children*. In relation to contact/access the matter has been taken further by the Report entitled *Transfrontier Access/Contact and Hague Convention of 25 October 1980 on the Civil Aspects of International Child Abduction* drawn up by William Duncan and described by him in Chapter 3.

There follow two contributions on the problems associated with children from the perspective of other jurisdictions.

In Chapter 4 Alastair Bissett-Johnson looks at recent developments and problems in Scotland in the area of child law. There are interesting contrasts between the development of the law relating to children's capacity in Scotland and developments in England and Wales. The Children (Scotland) Act 1995 goes further than English law in spelling out parental responsibilities and rights. The Scottish Children's Hearing system is, of course, well known for its informal disposition of cases involving children. Recent developments in this area are considered particularly in the light of the impact of the Human Rights Act 1998. Most family law in Scotland, with some important exceptions such as child support, is within the jurisdiction of the Scottish Parliament rather than the Westminster Parliament. The impact of the 1998 Act appears therefore to be more complicated than it is in England.

Brigitte Clark's chapter looks at responses to the immense problem of child poverty in South Africa. The size of the problem is staggering and the situation has been exacerbated by the impact of HIV/AIDS. The lack of resources to deal with the problem is a matter of great concern in South Africa, but it seems that the law may prove to be a significant factor in forcing the Government to take more dramatic action. The United Nations Convention on the Rights of the Child, ratified by South Africa, and the provisions of the South African Constitution, especially those relating to rights to social security and social services, seem to form an important foundation for action to alleviate child poverty. Three decisions of the South African courts which have built on this foundation are noted. The landmark decision of the Constitutional Court of South Africa in *The Government of the Republic of South Africa v. Grootboom and Others*[2] acknowledged the need for the South African government to develop a policy to ensure that every effort is made to comply with such rights and that socio-economic rights are justiciable in South Africa. This has been followed by a further decision of the court in an action by the Treatment Action Campaign regarding the provision of the anti-retroviral drug Nevirapine to HIV positive pregnant women.[3] Thirdly, a decision of the Supreme Court of Appeal in *The Permanent Secretary, Department of Welfare, Eastern Cape Government v. Ngxuza*[4] may prove an important step in the possible development of some form of class action on behalf of children deprived of any form of maintenance.

David Pearl is concerned with an important development in relation to decision making in the field of care. The need to protect children from unacceptable behaviour by an adult is especially important in relation to professionals or volunteers in child centred occupations. However, decisions taken to protect the welfare of children considered to be at risk may result in teachers, social workers and others working with children being barred from working in their chosen occupation. The tension that has always existed between the interests of children and the interests of such persons has been highlighted by the implementation of the Human Rights Act and the consequent need to ensure that administrative decision making is compliant with the European Convention. David Pearl describes the machinery that has now been put in place in England and Wales to hear appeals

---

[2]   2001 (1) SA 46 (CC).
[3]   *Minister of Health and Others v. Treatment Action Campaign and Others* 2002 (5) SA 721 (CC).
[4]   2001 (4) SA 1184 (SCA).

from those individuals who have been prohibited from working with children. The Care Standards Tribunal came into existence in England and Wales from April 1, 2002. It incorporates two existing tribunals, the old Registered Homes Tribunal and the newly created Protection of Children Act Tribunal. The new Tribunal has an important role not merely in relation to decisions in individual cases, but in providing guidance that will help in the formulation of standards in this sensitive area.

Chapter 7 is the first of two chapters concerned with the relationship between the family and property. It is to be expected that the law relating to inheritance in any particular society will reflect that society's view of the family.[5] Thus in common law countries generally the law of intestate succession has developed so as to reflect the claims of the nuclear family rather than the wider family and within the nuclear family, the claims of a surviving spouse have achieved greater emphasis at the expense of the claims of the children. Prue Vines is concerned with the application of the statutory and common law regimes to Aboriginal people and Torres Strait Islanders in Australia. She sets out and examines a number of myths relating to Aboriginal people and the impact those myths have had on the application of those regimes to aboriginal people. She then looks at the more accurate picture which can be ascertained from the available evidence and outlines the regimes with particular emphasis on those which have been developed to apply to 'traditional' Aboriginal people. She argues that there are significant problems with all the regimes which apply to Aboriginal people on intestacy even though some regimes are represented as recognising customary law. In particular there is a failure to recognise the different kinship patterns of Aboriginal people and Torres Strait Islanders and their impact in inheritance law.

There is no easy solution to the problems. It is obviously important to recognise customary law in inheritance and some legislative change is desirable. The kinship group entitled on inheritance should be extended to one matching customary law patterns and there should be a similar extension of those eligible to apply for family provision. Intestate succession provides certainty but it does not provide the flexibility necessary in relation to different kinds of property. Family provision legislation can provide the necessary degree of flexibility, but it may require a court hearing and involves costs. However, she concludes that the best way of ensuring protection and enforcement of customary law in relation to inheritance is the making of wills which recognise Aboriginal customary law.

The final chapter is concerned with pre-nuptial agreements. Agreements between spouses in relation to financial and property matters following the breakdown of their marriage have now become commonplace. Since the reform of divorce law by the Divorce Reform Act 1969 such agreements have no longer run the risk of being regarded as part of a 'collusive' bargain. On the contrary they are encouraged in what has been called the 'settlement culture'[6] which is now a well

---

[5] As Professor Plucknett pointed out "The law of succession is an attempt to express the family in terms of property". *A Concise History of the Common Law* 4th Ed. (1948) p.673.

[6] Davis, Cretney and Collins, *Simple Quarrels* (1994) p.211.

established feature of the divorce process. They cannot oust the jurisdiction of the court, but they carry great weight when the courts come to exercise their discretionary powers to make orders for financial provision and property adjustment. In contrast agreements made before marriage by prospective spouses have not achieved the same degree of recognition. Such agreements remain 'unenforceable' as such in English law, but the courts are increasingly having to consider the weight to be attached to such agreements which have been entered into abroad and, more recently, in England. Moreover, other legal systems, including those in the common law world, have introduced legislation according recognition to pre-nuptial agreements and the government has lent support to such recognition being introduced into English law. This chapter considers the arguments for and against recognition after looking at the different meanings which may be attributed to 'recognition' in this context in the light of the approaches adopted to pre-nuptial agreements in England and their jurisdictions.

Chapter 1

The Changed Nature of Adoption: A Challenge for the Legislators

Caroline Ball

Introduction

Adoption, a legal order effecting the irrevocable transfer of a child from one family to another, is a familiar concept. For all those involved in the so-called 'adoption triangle', the process is to a greater or lesser extent bound to be one in which deep emotions, uncertainty and unresolved conflicts are experienced. The law can only regulate the process, but in doing so it provides the framework within which difficult decisions involving children's lives and complex personal sensitivities are taken. The regulation of adoption has to achieve a delicate balance that places the child's welfare throughout life at the heart of decision making, and at the same time is fair to all the parties. For more than a decade it has been apparent that because of the changed nature of adoption practice, regulation of the process under the Adoption Act 1976 no longer meets these basic requirements.

The long overdue Adoption and Children Act 2002, replacing the 1976 Act, is likely to be fully implemented in 2004. Reforms after the introduction of legal adoption in 1926 and prior to 1975 were largely concerned with regulating the process of adoption to eliminate perceived abuses,[1] and with equating the adopted child's legal status within the adoptive family more closely with that of birth children for the purposes of inheritance.[2] At the beginning of the 21st century the context is very different. Since 1976, the nature of adoption has altered to such an extent that a much more radical reform of its regulation is required than has been the case in the past. This chapter will consider, within the context of societal and practice changes, the themes that dominate the reforms and attempt critical evaluation of the extent to which the Act responds to the changed nature of adoptive relationships.[3]

---

[1]   Adoption of Children (Regulation) Act 1939.
[2]   Adoption of Children Act 1949.
[3]   N. Lowe, *The changing face of adoption - the gift/donation model versus the contract/services model* (1997) 9 C. F. L. Q. 371.

Adoption: the first 50 years

There were two main policy imperatives behind the introduction of legal adoption in 1927: the need for recognition of the many *de facto* adoptions in existence, and the encouragement of the provision of family life for large numbers of illegitimate children and orphans who would otherwise be likely to spend their childhood in institutions. *De facto* adoptions, in which children were brought up outside their birth families by agreement were commonplace but existed without any security for the arrangement. Without recourse to costly and risky litigation, the people who had raised the child were unable to resist demands by birth parents for return, often at a time when the child was old enough to contribute to family finances. The 1920s saw increased professional interest in children's welfare and recognition that allowing the early adoption of illegitimate babies would spare children both the bleak reality of life in an institution and the stigma of illegitimacy. This led to the setting up of many charitable agencies arranging placements of babies in parallel to the increase in the number of *de facto* adoptions of orphans and abandoned children by relatives and strangers which followed the First World War. Pressure grew for the legalisation of adoption, to remedy the weaknesses inherent in *de facto* arrangements and with the additional benefit that the creation of new, secure, nuclear families would relieve many infertile couples from the misery of childlessness.

Despite the strength of the case made by protagonists and the fact that legal adoption, long embedded in legal systems based on Roman Law, had by that time been introduced in many other common law jurisdictions, opposition to legal adoption was deeply entrenched in a property oriented psyche. This is well illustrated by the early 1920s response of Edward Manson, a barrister, to a query from an academic in New York researching the law of adoption.

> The law of England knows nothing of adoption. Its theory is that the father, as legal guardian - and the same principle applies to the mother - cannot abdicate by any contract the position of parental responsibility, or rid himself irrevocably of the sacred duties of fatherhood. He may purport to do so, but the law will not recognise any such promise as binding; it allows him to retract and repudiate it at any time.[4]

Such was the weight of opposition in the House of Lords that it was only after reports from two departmental committees,[5] which both favoured the introduction of legal adoption, though for disparate reasons and in differing forms, and several failed Bills, that the Adoption of Children Act 1926 finally reached the statute book. Implemented in 1927, it introduced an order effecting the complete and irrevocable transfer of the child from the birth family to the adopters for all purposes apart from succession.

---

[4]   J.F. Brosnan, *The Law of Adoption* (1922) Columbia L. R. 332, at p.335.
[5]   Report of the *Committee on Child Adoption* (Chair, Sir Alfred Hopkinson K.C.) 1921, Cmd. 125, London: HMSO; Report of *The Child Adoption Committee* (Chair, Tomlin J.) 1925, Cmd. 2401, London: HMSO.

Adoption practice

Contrary to expectations prior to legalisation in 1926,[6] adoption proved popular. There was a steady rise in the number of orders, with unsurprising and erratic surges during the 1939–45 war, from nearly 3,000 orders in 1927 to a high of 24,831 in 1968. The vast majority of orders during this period were so-called private law adoptions of illegitimate babies or young children by strangers, or their own children by parents (generally mothers) often with a step-parent.[7] At that time, only a minute proportion, 3.2 per cent in 1952, were adopted out of local authority care.[8]

During this period, adoption law developed in a way that increasingly, through mechanisms that cloaked the process in secrecy, separated the child for all time and for all purposes from his or her birth family, providing corresponding security within the adoptive family.[9] Effectively law and practice encouraged the fiction that the adopted child's birth family did not exist and many people adopted as babies grew up not knowing, often until late in life, that they were adopted.[10]

The winds of change

In-country adoption   Adoption statistics, beyond the numbers of orders made annually and even they are somewhat unreliable, are woefully inadequate. Because of the failure to collect and record essential data, many of the vital questions properly asked by researchers and policy makers remain unanswered and unanswerable.[11] Despite this, and some disparity between the numbers of adoption orders recorded according to the source of the statistics,[12] there is no doubt about the overall trends over the last 75 years.

After the high watermark of 1968, for a variety of well-explored reasons relating to the legalisation of abortion,[13] changing attitudes to illegitimacy, and the

6   The *Child Adoption* Committee (1925) chaired by Tomlin J. demonstrated a negative attitude towards adoption in its first report, Cmd. 2401, at para. 4.
7   J. Masson , D. Norbury and S. Chatterton (1983) *Mine, Yours or Ours?*, London: HMSO.
8   N. Lowe (2000) *English Adoption Law: Past, Present, and Future* in *Cross Currents* (Ed., S.N. Katz, J. Eekelaar and M. Maclean), Oxford: OUP.
9   The Adoption of Children (Regulation) Act, 1939 and the Adoption of Children Act 1949 were consolidated, together with remaining provisions of the Adoption of Children Act 1926 and the Adoption of Children (Scotland) Act 1930 into the Adoption Act 1950. The Adoption Act 1958 introduced major reforms and was followed by minor amendments in the Adoption Acts 1960, 1964 and 1968.
10   Kormitzer (1968) *Adoption and Family Life*, London: Putnam.
11   Fruin (1980) *Sources of Statistical Information on Adoption*, Adoption and Fostering, No. 100; C. Dance (1997) *Focus on Adoption: A snapshot of adoption patterns in England - 1995*, London: BAAF; J.Triseliotis, J. Shireman and M. Hundleby (1997) *Adoption: theory, policy and practice*, London: Cassell: BAAF, (1996).
12   Department of Health, 1999.
13   Abortion Act 1967.

availability of welfare benefits and housing for single mothers, the number of illegitimate babies available for adoption in the United Kingdom declined very rapidly. From a peak of nearly 25,000, the number of adoption orders made annually fell to just over 10,500 in 1980, 6,500 in 1990, and just under 4,500 in 2000 (slightly more than in 1999).[14] Over the same period, the age of children when the order was made continued to rise reflecting the shift away from baby adoption. Figures in the 1993 white paper *Adoption: the future* indicate that the number of babies under 12 months fell from 23 per cent of the total of nearly 13,000 children adopted in 1977 to 12 per cent of the just over 7000 children adopted in 1991.[15] The proportion of older children (1–17) had risen from 77 per cent to 88 per cent. The somewhat convoluted way in which the comparisons are presented in the white paper reflects the lack of detail available. Although the 1977 figures divided the older children into 1–14 and 15–17 year olds, even that distinction could not be drawn from the 1991 data.

Intercountry adoption   As the supply of babies dwindled in all Western European and other developed countries across the world, and especially after the revolutions in Eastern Europe, childless couples increasingly looked to poor countries in South America and Asia as well as Eastern Europe, where there was a ready supply of babies who without adoption faced a bleak future. In 1991, UNICEF estimated that in developing countries 155 million children under five lived in absolute poverty and the Secretary General of International Social Service referred to over 100 million children being abandoned to subsist by providing cheap labour or engaging in petty crime or prostitution.[16] Since then, population control policies have led to the abandonment to orphanage life of thousands of female babies in China. As Triseliotis identifies, in the growth of intercountry adoption initially compassion and humanitarianism went side by side with the wish to create or expand a family. As the supply of babies to adopt in-country declined, 'the latter came to predominate', leading to the growth of a global trade in children, driven more by market forces than the rights and needs of children.[17]

The changed adoptive population

From the late 1970s, local authority child care practice, helped by greater powers to carry out plans based on 'permanence' for children in long term care provided by the Children Act 1975, increasingly saw adoption as a solution for children across the age range unable to be rehabilitated within their birth families.[18] Despite

---

14   Lord Chancellor's Department, *Judicial Statistics* (2000), London: The Stationery Office.

15   Department of Health (1993) Cm. 2288, HMSO, Chapter 3.

16   W. Duncan (1993) *Regulating Intercountry Adoption* in *Frontiers of Family Law*, 2nd edition, Bainham, Pearl and Pickford eds., Chichester: John Wiley.

17   J. Triseliotis (2000) *Intercountry Adoption: Global Trade or Global Gift* 24 Adoption and Fostering at 48.

18   J. Thoburn, A. Murdoch and A. O'Brien (1986) *Permanence in Child Care*, Oxford: Basil Blackwell.

local authorities becoming adoption agencies with duties in regard to the provision of services to support adoption, and the introduction of allowances to encourage the adoption of children classified on account of age or disability as 'hard to place', outcomes were not encouraging. It is known that many of these placements, especially of older children, many of whom had had damaging experiences of family life and therefore brought a burden of emotional baggage and past relationships with them, broke down. When this happened, the children returned to care, leaving at the age of 18 with no family support.[19]

Since there is no general agreement as to what constitutes breakdown or disruption in long-term foster care or adoption, it is perhaps understandable that no official statistics are gathered on the breakdown of placements, either before or after the making of the order.[20] There is little doubt, however, that the consequence was a lack of detailed qualitative research into the making and support of placements to inform policies and practice. The late 1980s and 1990s saw attempts to remedy this deficit.

Post-adoption contact   The New Zealand concept of 'open adoption' in which the birth family continue to have considerable involvement in the child's life after the adoption order is made was alien to adoption practice in the United Kingdom. Despite the courts having the power to attach any conditions to an adoption order, including orders for continuing contact, few orders were made though there were exceptions. As early as 1973, in *Re J (A Minor)(Adoption Order: Conditions)*[21] Rees J. made a condition of access by a birth parent to an adopted child in order to avoid lengthy litigation which would have been damaging to the child. It is perhaps indicative of the strength of the courts' reluctance to fetter the autonomy of the adoptive family in any way that it was another 16 years before the decision in *Re J* was confirmed by the House of Lords in *Re C (A Minor)(Adoption Order: Conditions)*[22] a case concerning contact between an adopted child and her sibling. Since the 1980s there has been an accelerating recognition that post-adoption contact with birth families or other significant people from the past has great value for some adopted children. A number of research studies support the conclusion that where the value of continuing contact, either face to face or through correspondence, is not only recognised but also facilitated, the children benefit both from the security of adoption and from an increased understanding of their own identity.[23]

---

[19]   J. Fratter, J. Rowe, D. Sapsford and J. Thoburn (1991) *Permanent Family Placement: a decade of experience*, London: BAAF.

[20]   J. Rowe, *Fostering Outcomes: Interpreting Breakdown Rates* (1987) 11 Adoption and Fostering 1.

[21]   [1973] 2 All E. R. 410.

[22]   [1989] A.C.1.

[23]   J. Fratter et al. op cit., n.19; J. Fratter (1996) *Adoption with Contact: Implications for Policy and Practice*, London: BAAF; Neil, E., *Contact with Birth Relatives After Adoption: a study of young recently placed children*, unpublished PhD thesis, University of East Anglia, 2000.

Changing the conceptual framework   Research funded by the Department of Health and undertaken in the mid 1990s by Lowe and Murch and their colleagues at Cardiff explored the policy and practice implications of the changed nature of the adoptive population through the experiences and perceptions of adults and children. Focusing on the adoption of older children out of local authority care, the aim of the study was to aid understanding of the challenges for the children and families involved.[24] The researchers identified an immensely wide range of practice in relation to all aspects of the process, and endemic delays within the courts. They concluded that essential to the reform of the regulation of adoption was recognition that the law needed to reflect the extent to which the whole nature of adoption had changed. Since 1926 practice had been predicated on what they term the gift/donation model in which the birth parent 'gives away' her baby via the adoption agency to the adopters, who having been exhaustively scrutinised as to their suitability, are then 'left to their own devices and resources to bring up the child as their own'.[25] This model, the one currently underpinned by the 1976 Act, does not fit the adoption of older children from care. In contrast the changed nature of adoption practice requires acceptance that 'adoption is not the end of the process but only a stage (albeit an important stage) in an ongoing and often complex process of family development'.[26] For this so called contract/service model to be effective, Lowe and Murch et al. suggest that the law relating to post-adoption support and the payment of adoption allowances needs substantial strengthening in recognition that services to support the adoption might well continue to be required throughout childhood.

Reforming the law for changed adoption practice

Informed by the recommendations of the Houghton Committee,[27] the statute currently regulating adoption, the Adoption Act 1976, consolidated reforms enacted in the Children Act 1975 with surviving provisions in the Adoption Act 1958[28] (which predated the decline in baby adoptions). The 1976 Act, for a variety of political and economic reasons was not fully implemented until 1988, by which time the changes in adoption practice had overtaken not only the long lasting provisions from earlier legislation, but also many of the reforms the 1975 Act introduced.

---

[24]   N. Lowe and M. Murch, M. Borkowski, A Weaver, V. Beckford and C. Thomas (1999) *Supporting Adoption: Reframing the Approach*, London: BAAF.

[25]   Ibid., at 429.

[26]   N. Lowe and M. Murch et al. op. cit. n.14.

[27]   Home Office and Scottish Education Department (1972) *Report of the Departmental Committee on the Adoption of Children*, Cmnd. 5107, London: HMSO.

[28]   As amended by the Adoption Acts 1960, 1964 and 1968.

The reform process

Throughout the 1980s all of public and private child law, apart from that relating to adoption, was the subject of unprecedented scrutiny in terms both of the substantive law and its impact on social workers' decision making.[29] By the end of the decade it was recognised that adoption law was as much in need of reform to meet the changed nature of adoption practice as the rest of child law. A year after the 1976 Act was finally fully implemented and in the same year that radical reform and some consolidation of the rest of child law was enacted in the Children Act 1989, a working group of departmental officials and a Law Commissioner was set up to review adoption law and report to ministers. The group, chaired by the civil servant who had led the Children Act 1989 team and working in a very similar way, produced working papers for consultation, commissioned background material and studied research reports. In 1992 the group published its report to ministers as a consultation document.[30]

In addition to the essential ingredients of making adoption a more child-centred process and regulating intercountry adoption, the 1992 review identified substantial areas of the current law as being in need of reform, either through amendment or innovation. Essentially the reformed legal framework would need to meet the needs of the diverse and complex population of children in the public care who are unable to return home and seek a family for life outside, but not necessarily totally cut off from, that into which they were born. The group's recommendations and the subsequent discourse can be encompassed within four key themes: the enhanced responsibilities of local authorities throughout the adoption process and beyond; eligibility to adopt; the rights of birth parents; and, the continuing place of birth families in the life of children who cannot return home.

Progress between the publication of the group's report in October 1992 and legislation proved slow. The foreword to the report contained the cautious and, it proved, prescient, caveat that 'Ministers are not committed to proceeding with any of the recommendations for change and will take decisions in the light of public responses and of the availability of resources'.[31] Clearly the working group members recognised that the need for reform was urgent, since they explicitly ruled out waiting to legislate until the effect of implementation of the Children Act 1989 could be judged, and agreement reached on the proposed Hague Convention on intercountry adoption. 'Our proposals are designed to improve the law in this country and do not depend on a new international convention which would take some years to be effective.'[32]

---

[29]   See for instance, Department of Health and Social Services (1985) *Social Work Decisions in Child Care*, London: HMSO; C. Ball (1990) *Children Act 1989: Issues, Aims and Current Concerns* in *Social Work and Social Welfare Year Book* 2, P. Carter, T Jeffs. and M. Smith (eds), pp.1-21, Open U P, 1990.

[30]   Department of Health and Welsh Office (1992) *Review of Adoption Law*, London: Department of Health.

[31]   Ibid., at i.

[32]   Ibid., at para. 1.8.

The proposed reforms included: the replacement of the freeing for adoption provisions with placement orders to be applied for by local authorities prior to making a permanent placement outside the birth family; a new order for *inter vivos* guardianship with more security than a residence order but without final legal severance from the birth family;[33] better post-adoption services; and a single ground for dispensing with parental consent.[34] The proposals were for the most part widely welcomed and were responded to by a wide range of child care agencies and organisations.[35] The consultation process was followed in 1993 by a substantially incomplete white paper, *Adoption – the future*[36] and two further consultation documents on the placement orders which would replace freeing for adoption. In March 1996 the government published for consultation a draft Bill under the title *Adoption: A Service for Children*, which incorporated the recently agreed Hague Convention on Intercountry Adoption with the other proposed reforms. This Bill differed in significant respects from the white paper proposals.[37] Whilst there was a substantial degree of support for much of its content, key provisions attracted considerable criticism.[38]

The Conservative government, with a very slender majority, was faced with opposition from its own right wing to the regulation of intercountry adoption through incorporation of the Hague Convention into domestic law. Many child care organisations also made clear their concerns over several clauses including the grounds for dispensing with parental consent, which differed significantly from that proposed in the *Review of Adoption Law,* and aspects of the new placement orders.[39] Faced with the prospect of contentious legislation, the government had no stomach for a fight and the draft Bill progressed no further. In the event this allowed the conclusions of the research into the adoption of older children from local authority care referred to above to inform the debate and subsequent legislation.

The Adoption and Children Bill

After the 1997 general election, adoption was not high on the agenda until the 'Quality Protects' programme identified as one of its aims the increased use of adoption for 'looked after' children who cannot live with their families (for whatever reason). Pressure was put on local authorities to get more 'looked after' children adopted through making an increase in numbers a performance indicator

---

[33]   Later named 'special guardianship' (Children Act 1989, s.14A-G).

[34]   In addition to the parent being unable to be found or incapable of giving consent.

[35]   British Association for Adoption and Fostering (1993) *The BAAF Response to the Review of Adoption Law*, London: BAAF.

[36]   Op. cit.

[37]   *Adoption: A Service for Children*, London: Department of Health.

[38]   C. Ball, *Adoption: A Service for Children?* (1996) 20 Adoption and Fostering 112–121.

[39]   See for instance *The BAAF Response to the Review of Adoption Law* (1993) London: BAAF.

of good practice.[40] The momentum for reform of the law was renewed, particularly in 2000 when the Prime Minister took a high-profile personal interest.[41] In the same year, the Adoption Law Reform Group, an informal network of several major child and family concerned organisations, initially convened by the British Agencies for Adoption and Fostering (BAAF) to share views on the principles which should underlie adoption, published its proposals for adoption law reform.[42] This paper, supported by the Association of Directors of Social Services (ADSS) set out the group's views on the main issues to be addressed in urgently needed new legislation.

A white paper *Adoption – a new approach*, which confusingly made reference to only a few of the areas of reform identified in all earlier proposals, was published by the Government immediately before Christmas 2000.[43] The Adoption and Children Bill, which incorporated the *Adoption – a new approach* proposals and many of those in the 1996 Bill, as well as introducing welcome amendments to the Children Act 1989, had its first reading in March 2001, but fell when Parliament was prorogued for the June general election.

The final lap

In October 2001, nine years after publication of the *Review of Adoption Law,* an amended version of the March Bill had its first reading. Again the Bill was widely welcomed, particularly as one of the main concerns relating to placement orders had been addressed by aligning the grounds for making the new orders with the threshold conditions for the making of a care or supervision order.[44] Debate during the remainder of the Bill's passage through Parliament was curtailed by a draconian timetable.

Adoption and Children Act 2002: the main reforms in context

Alignment with the Children Act 1989

The Act makes the child's welfare the paramount consideration of agencies and courts making decisions relating to adoption. In the same way that the so called 'welfare checklist' in the 1989 Act, s.1(3) provides an *aide memoire* for courts in regard to the issues they should consider when reaching a decision about the care or upbringing of a child, so section 1(4) sets out similar adoption related issues to

40   Department of Health (1999) *The Government's Objectives for Children's Social Services,* London: Department of Health, performance Indicator C23 at para. 1.3.
41   Policy Innovations Unit, *Prime Minister's Review of Adoption,* Cabinet Office, (2000).
42   Adoption Law Reform Group, (2000) *Reforming Adoption Law in England and Wales,* London: BAAF.
43   Cm. 5017. For a critique, see C. Ball, *The White Paper, Adoption: a new approach – A Curate's Egg?* (2001) 25, Adoption and Fostering 6 – 12.
44   Children Act 1989, s.31(2).

which agencies and courts must pay regard. The list includes the child's wishes and feelings, the likely effect of adoption on the child throughout life, [45] and consideration of likely continuing relationships with relatives or others.

The responsibilities of local authorities

The gradual professionalisation of the adoption process and the increased role played by local authorities can be traced as a dominant theme discernable since early amendments to the Adoption and Children Act 1926. Professionalisation accelerated with the appointment of qualified children's officers in local authorities following the Children Act 1948, and was effectively completed in the adoption provisions in the Children Act 1975. It was only in that Act that placements for adoption by parents (except with relatives) and by third parties such as the vicar or the general practitioner were outlawed. [46] Placing for adoption was recognised as being an activity requiring professional judgement in the selection of suitable families for children seeking an adoptive placement. Judgement that in the interests of the child should only be exercised by an approved adoption agency worker (although until very recently many agency workers lacked professional qualifications). In the same Act provisions were introduced requiring all local authorities to become adoption agencies, with responsibility for providing services 'designed to meet the needs, in relation to adoption of –

(a)   children who have or may be adopted,
(b)   parents and guardians of such children, and
(c)   persons who have adopted or may adopt a child,

and for that purpose to provide the requisite facilities, or secure that they are provided by approved adoption agencies'. [47] As the number of children adopted from care grew, given token help by the power given to local authorities under the 1976 Act to provide allowances to support the adoption of 'hard to place' children, [48] the adoption work of local authorities expanded in volume and in complexity.

---

[45]   Previous legislation made reference only to the child's welfare throughout childhood. The new test recognises that decisions taken in childhood have consequences throughout life.

[46]   Considerable efforts had been made by professionals involved with adoption to persuade the earlier *Departmental Committee on the Adoption of Children*, (Chair, Sir Gerald Hurst Q.C.) Cmd. 9248, London: HMSO, which reported in 1954, to impose similar restrictions. The Committee recognised that some direct and third party placements were unsatisfactory, but were not convinced of the need to outlaw them, nor confident, given the number of such placements made, that Adoption Agencies could handle the demands that would be placed upon them.

[47]   Adoption Act 1976, s.1(1).

[48]   Means testing for adoption allowances acted as a deterrent to adoption for some families who could not afford to adopt rather than continue to receive non-means-tested boarding out allowances for foster children.

Many of the children for whom adoptive homes are now sought have been deeply damaged both by experiences within their birth families and by many moves in care and delays in the adoption process. As a consequence, many suffer a range of emotional and behavioural disabilities which place heavy demands on the adoptive families. Research referred to above[49] showed that the range and quality of supportive services provided by local authorities as adoption agencies, especially in regard to the adoptive family after the order was made, was very variable, and on-going support was in some cases critical to prevent the breakdown of the adoptive relationship.[50] The researchers also identified the random nature of the payment of adoption allowances and the extent to which children and adoptive families were disadvantaged by such allowances being paid at a lower rate than for fostering.

The new Act requires local authorities to provide support services, including financial assistance, before, during, and after adoption for children, birth families and adopters, and to assess the needs of individuals requesting services. Unfortunately there is no duty on the local authority to provide the services if the assessment suggests that they are required.[51] Nor, until regulations are published, will it be clear how the new system of adoption allowances will work.

Eligibility to adopt

The Adoption Act 1976 was in the main predicated on adoption practice as it existed until the early 1970s, that is to say the adoption of mainly, healthy, white, illegitimate babies by childless married couples; demand always outstripping supply. In contrast, at the present time the majority of the adoptive population are older, often deeply damaged, children in the public care for whom return to their birth family is not possible. Adopting a looked after child often demands of the adopters an extraordinary degree of commitment and resilience to deal with challenging behaviour, making suitable prospective adopters hard to find especially for sibling groups. It is hardly surprising that local authorities now always have more children for whom they are seeking adoptive homes, than suitable prospective adopters.[52]

Since 1998 it has been Government policy to promote and increase adoption into a loving, stable home for looked after children unable to return to their birth families.[53] In furtherance of this policy a target has been set to increase these adoptions by 40 per cent by 2004/5.[54] It therefore seems paradoxical that during most of the Bill's passage through the House of Commons, ministers demonstrated an entrenched reluctance to relax the existing rule that only single people or married couples could adopt a child. Under the 1976 Act, where a child seeking

---

[49]   N. Lowe and M. Murch et al. op. cit. n.15.
[50]   Ibid., at Chapter 12.
[51]   Adoption and Children Act 2002, s.4(4).
[52]   D. Howe (1998) *Patterns of Adoption*, Oxford: Blackwell Science; N. Lowe et al. op.cit. n. 14.
[53]   Department of Health, *Achieving the Right Balance*, LAC (1998) 20.
[54]   *Adoption: a new approach*, Cm. 5017, London: The Stationery Office.

adoption is placed with an unmarried couple, however stable their relationship and however committed they are to adoption, only one of them can become the child's legal parent through adoption – the child being deprived of the legal and lifetime commitment that only joint adoption could bring. Research showed that this has discouraged otherwise suitable couples, who for one reason or another were not married to each other, from applying to adopt. The British Agencies for Adoption and Fostering (BAAF) estimated that the pool of prospective adopters could be enlarged by as much as 20 per cent if the law were changed to allow unmarried couples to adopt.

Well orchestrated pressure from almost all the leading child welfare agencies finally persuaded the Government to reconsider its position and at third reading in the Commons a free vote was allowed on an amendment which was passed by a very substantial majority, several Conservative members either absenting themselves or defying a three line whip to oppose the amendment.[55] A subsequent opposition amendment to exclude same sex couples from the provision failed.[56] After a passionate debate in the House of Lords, the requirement that a couple could only adopt a child jointly if married to each other was removed at the Report stage.[57] The Lords amendment was reversed by the Commons, a decision subsequently supported in the House of Lords, when many peers who had previously voted against reform changed their minds. As a result there will be no bar to heterosexual unmarried couples or same sex couples, who pass the usual rigorous assessment procedures as to their suitability, jointly adopting a child.

Step-parent adoptions

By the time the Houghton Committee started its work in 1969 very large numbers of children were being adopted jointly by a parent, usually the mother, and a step-parent. Many of these children had been born to single mothers, but an increasing number had been born to parents who subsequently divorced, and a small minority had lost a parent through death. This use of adoption was not contemplated in the first Adoption Act in 1926, but developed opportunistically as a means of achieving legitimate status for children born outside marriage and rapidly became popular.[58] This despite the fact that the process involved the mother having to adopt her own child. By the 1960s some social workers, probation officers and judges were questioning whether children's welfare was well served by the legal severance from half of their birth family bought about by step-parent adoption following divorce or the remarriage of a widowed parent. In its 1969 report *Adoption: The Way Ahead* the Association of Child Care Officers suggested that instead of adoption, step-parents should be able to acquire guardian status. The Houghton Committee endorsed this view to the extent that guardianship should be the preferred alternative, though evidence they received convinced them that adoption should remain a possibility.

55 Hansard H.C. Vol 385. No. 149, 1004 - 1007.
56 Ibid. Vol. 386, No. 150, 92 - 95.
57 Hansard H.L. Vol. 639, 864 - 913.
58 Masson et al., op cit.

A guardianship order would differ from an adoption order in that it would not be irrevocable, would not permanently extinguish parental rights, would not alter the child's relationship to the members of his natural family or extinguish his right to inherit from them.[59]

In the event, guardianship was abandoned and the 1975 Act provisions discouraged step-parent adoption by requiring, in the case of previously married parents, consideration of the variation of an existing custody order in favour of the step-parent.[60] Where there was no previous marriage, step-parents could apply for the newly introduced custodianship order which had the same effect.

When these provisions were first introduced in 1976 there was an assumption that step-parent adoptions would end. The assumption proved false. After a few judicial decisions made it clear that the ban was not absolute,[61] the number of step-parent adoptions increased again though never to the levels prior to the Children Act 1975. The actual extent of the increase cannot be measured owing to the available statistics not differentiating between step-parent and stranger adoptions between 1983 and 1992. In 1998 judicial statistics suggest that step-parent adoptions accounted for about half of all adoption orders.[62]

Following a similar provision in the 1996 Adoption Bill,[63] section 111 of the 2002 Act amends section 4 of the Children Act 1989 to enable a step-parent to acquire parental responsibility for his spouse's child by agreement with the birth parents or order of the court.[64] The new order, which will not end the parental responsibility of the absent parent has been widely welcomed as a desirable alternative to step-parent adoption. Where a step-parent acquires parental responsibility under section 4A, children will continue to be a part of their birth family and will inherit only from the birth parents or through a will.

The parental responsibility of a step-parent will not end automatically on divorce from the child's parent, but can be ended by a court on the application of any person with parental responsibility or, with leave, the child.[65]

Consent to adoption and the rights of birth parents

This recurrent theme has two main strands which are in practice often entwined but are also conceptually separate. Parental consent, freely given with understanding of the consequences of the order, has always been a legal requirement for adoption.[66]

---

59   Home Office and Scottish Education Department (1972), op.cit., n. 23, para. 123.
60   Children Act 1975, s. 10(3).
61   See for example, *Re D (Minors)(Adoption by a Step-Parent)* [1980] 2 F.L.R. 102, in which the Court of Appeal held that dismissal of the application was only required if it could be shown that the matter could better be dealt with by a joint custody order.
62   N. Lowe, op. cit., n.11.
63   Clause 85.
64   Children Act 1989, s.4A.
65   Ibid, s.4A (3).
66   The consent of unmarried fathers who have not acquired parental responsibility is not required.

The power of a court to dispense with parental consent, provided statutory criteria are satisfied, has also been a feature of adoption law since 1926. Based on the Houghton Committee's recommendations,[67] the Children Act 1975 introduced a radical reform which for the first time allowed the issue of consent to be dealt with separately from the making of the adoption order.[68] The new Act substantially alters the grounds for dispensing with parental consent and replaces the freeing for adoption procedure for determining consent issues in advance of the adoption application with placement by consent and placement orders.

Parental consent   Under the Adoption Act 1976, before an adoption order can be made the court has to be satisfied that the child has been freed for adoption (see below) or that every parent with parental responsibility freely gives their consent to the child's adoption.[69] The consent of parents with parental responsibility can only be dispensed with if one of the grounds set out in section 16(2) is satisfied. In the late 1980s it was estimated that nearly 20 per cent of adoptions involved dispensing with parental agreement.[70] The most commonly used and widely criticised of these grounds is that the parent is 'withholding his agreement unreasonably'.[71] In the Adoption Law Review, the Committee recognised that application of this provision is deeply unsatisfactory. It generally results in the court's view of reasonable refusal to consent being substituted for that of the parents, with the parents acquiring the stigma of being unreasonable. The Committee recognised that removing a parent's right to refuse to consent to their child's adoption is such a grave decision that it is the one matter that should not simply be made subject to the principle that the child's welfare is paramount. Instead it was recommended that in addition to the existing ground that 'the parent cannot be found or is incapable of giving agreement',[72] where a parent capable of giving consent can be found and is withholding agreement, a single test should replace all the other grounds.

> The test should require the court to be satisfied that the advantages to the child of becoming part of a new family are so significantly greater than the advantages to the child of any alternative option as to justify overriding the wishes of a parent or guardian.[73]

The 1996 draft Bill ignored the Committee's reasoning and introduced, in addition to the parent not being able to be found or being unable to give consent, a blanket ground for dispensing with parental consent: 'the court is satisfied that the welfare of the child requires the consent to be dispensed with'. This approach, which fails

67 Home Office and Scottish Education Department (1972), op. cit., n.19., Chapter 8.
68 Adoption Act 1976, s.18.
69 s. 16.
70 M. Murch, N. Lowe, M. Borkowski, R. Copner and K. Griew, (1993) *Pathways to Adoption*, London: HMSO.
71 s.16(2)(b).
72 Adoption Act 1976, s.16(2)(a).
73 Department of Health and Welsh Office (1992) *Review of Adoption Law*, London: Department of Health, at 4.

to recognise the gravity of a decision which irrevocably terminates a parent's legal relationship with his or her child, was widely criticised at the time.[74] The argument that it is the same ground as for other orders under the Children Act 1989, ignores the finality of adoption as compared with a residence order or even a care order, both of which may be revoked and neither of which remove parental responsibility from the parent(s). In addition, European Court of Human Rights jurisprudence suggests that the 'welfare of the child' test may be vulnerable to challenge under the Human Rights Act 1998 as being in breach of the right to family life under Article 8 of the European Convention on Human Rights. Decisions in Strasbourg endorse the need for exceptional circumstances to justify permanent severance of the parent-child relationship.[75]

No reference at all was made to this difficult and important element of adoption law in the 2000 white paper, *Adoption: a new approach.*[76] Through the passage of both Bills which followed, despite determined efforts being made to persuade the Government to adopt the test recommended by the 1992 Committee, which was wholeheartedly endorsed by the Adoption Law Reform Group in 2000,[77] and concerted lobbying of members of both Houses, no changes were made.

Separation of parental consent from the making of the adoption order   In the very small number of cases of babies being relinquished for adoption at an early stage, the freeing for adoption procedures in the 1976 Act appear to have worked in the way the Houghton Committee intended.[78] However, the 1992 report identified the extent to which the freeing for adoption provisions were proving unsatisfactory in cases in which parents were refusing their consent to adoption and local authorities were seeking freeing orders in advance of identifying prospective adopters.[79] Many freed children were left in a legal limbo when placements were not made or broke down, as is evidenced by the number and variety of cases in which Family Division judges have had to invoke the inherent jurisdiction in order to get round the statutory provisions (See for example: *Re G (Adoption: Freeing Order);*[80] *Re J (Freeing for Adoption);*[81] *Re C (Adoption: Freeing Order)*[82]). At the same time parents wishing to contest applications to dispense with their consent to the child's adoption are deeply disadvantaged by delays in the system which allow

---

74   B. Lindley and N. Wyld, *The Children Act and the draft Adoption Bill - diverging principles?* (1996) 8 C.F.L.Q. 327.
75   Per *Soderbac v Sweden* (Commission 22 October 1997 E.H.R.R.; *Johansen v. Norway* [1996] 23 E.H.R.R. 33.
76   Op. cit.
77   Adoption Law Reform Group, *Reforming Adoption Law in England and Wales,* BAFF (2000).
78   Department of Health (1992) *Review of Adoption Law,* op. cit. at para. 14.9: 'It is important ... that there should continue to be a provision for birth mothers who have chosen to have a child adopted to end their involvement in the adoption process at an early stage.'
79   Ibid., paras. 14.3 - 14.5.
80   [1997] 2 F.L.R. 202.
81   [2000] 2 F.L.R. 58.
82   [1999] 1 F.L.R. 348.

their children to become well established within other families before the parents have any opportunity to challenge the local authority's plan for the child before a court.[83]

The 1992 report proposed placement orders, to be applied for prior to the child being placed, as an alternative to freeing orders. Local authorities would have to seek such an order before making the placement, thus allowing the parents to contest plans for the adoption of their children at an early stage. The initial proposals and the provisions in the 1996 draft Bill proved contentious and were the subject of considerable debate, particularly since the criteria proposed for the making a placement order, which could result in the final legal severance of the child from the birth family through adoption, were considerable less stringent than the threshold conditions for the making of a care order.[84] The January 2001 Bill failed to address these concerns, though by the time the second Bill was introduced the strength of the case had been recognised and the criteria for the making of a placement order had been aligned with the threshold conditions in section 31(2) of the Children Act 1989.

Throughout the passage of the Bill, many details of the complex placement order provisions continued to be debated and amended. Amendments proposed by BAAF and the Family Rights Group, with widespread professional support, which would have considerably simplified the provisions by requiring a placement order in all cases, were rejected. Complex provisions in Chapter 3 of the Act provide for placement by consent as well as placement orders in contested cases.

The continuing place of birth families in the lives of children

Contact   Despite the apparent advantages identified by researchers, until recently post adoption contact remained a contentious issue involving deep sensitivities and disagreements about the principles underlying contact.[85] However, attitudes are changing. The 2001 National Adoption Standards for England address contact in Section A.

10.   The child's needs, wishes and feelings, and their welfare and safety are the most important concerns when considering links or contact with birth parents, wider family members and other people who are significant to them.

11.   Adoption plans will include details of the arrangements for maintaining links (including contact) with birth parents, wider birth family members and other people who are significant to the child and how and when these arrangements will be reviewed.

The National Standards are underpinned in the welfare checklist in the 2002 Act which requires agencies and courts reaching decisions relating to the adoption of a child to have regard to the relationship which the child has with relatives, and

---

83   M. Murch and N. Lowe et al. (1993), op. cit. n.59.
84   Children Act 1989, s. 31(2).
85   N. Lowe and M. Murch et al. (1999), op cit, n.14, Chapter 15.

others, including 'the likelihood of any such relationship continuing and the value to the child of its doing so'.[86] In the main continuing contact, if appropriate, will be arranged without a court order, however if an order is required it can be made at the time of the adoption order or subsequently under section 8 of the Children Act 1989. Separate contact order provisions apply to placement orders.[87]

Special guardianship   The inter-departmental working party reporting in 1992 suggested that for some older children who maintained meaningful links with a birth family to whom they would be very unlikely to return, the finality of the legal severance from that family through adoption was not appropriate. On the other hand, some greater security than that provided by a residence order which would only give the carers limited parental responsibility and would end at the age of 16 or 18 at the latest, was required. The group's proposals for an *inter vivos* guardianship order did not appear in the 1996 draft Bill, but reappeared, renamed, as 'special guardianship' in the 2000 white paper, *Adoption: a new approach.*[88] Section 115 of the 2002 Act inserts very detailed provisions in sections 14A - G of the Children Act 1989. Special guardians exercise parental responsibility to the exclusion of anyone else, but birth parents do not lose theirs, and there may be orders for continuing contact. There is also provision for local authority support services for special guardians. It is unclear whether special guardianship orders will be made, but for some children, the order provides the flexibility to ensure the security of the placement, whilst maintaining legal links with their birth family.

Conclusion

Until the 1980s, the secrecy surrounding the adoption process effectively barred all but relatively small scale research, mostly relying on anecdotal evidence, into the experience and outcomes of the irrevocable transfer of a child from one family to another for the parties involved. Earlier reform of adoption law could not rely on research, but in the main responded to the evidence of professionals and representatives from voluntary and statutory agencies regarding alleged deficits and abuses existing under current legislation. This time, the context of the reforms is different. In the same way that the provisions of the Children Act 1989 were informed by large-scale Department of Health funded research undertaken in the late 1970s and 1980s, so the Adoption and Children Act 2002 has benefited from the opening up of the process and its impact on individuals to research. Despite this, as for the most part well-informed debates during the progress of the Bill through Parliament have demonstrated, adoption remains an area of deep complexity and sensitivity for which the blunt instrument of legislation is unlikely ever to be able to provide all the answers.

---

[86]   Adoption and Children Act 2002, s.1(4)(f)(ii).

[87]   Ibid, s. 26.

[88]   Cm. 5017, London: The Stationery Office.

Chapter 2

Contact after Divorce: What has the Law to Offer?

Liz Trinder

Introduction

In this chapter I want to explore the relationship between two significant trends in family law. The first is the move to the promotion of private ordering to settle family disputes. Both the Children Act 1989 and the ill-fated Family Law Act 1996 are based on the presumption that where possible parents rather than the courts are the best people to decide post-divorce arrangements for children and consequently the active involvement of the courts or judicial determination should be restricted to those cases where parents cannot agree.[1] The second major trend is the emergence of a strong although rebuttable legal presumption in favour of contact between children and non-resident parents after divorce. Case law since implementation of the Children Act 1989 has arguably elevated the presumption of contact to a 'legal rule'[2] and the Family Law Act 1996 contained the first statutory although rebuttable presumption of contact.[3]

Both trends or principles have been subject to sustained criticism. Some have argued that the emphasis on parental agreement diminishes the role of law as external arbiter or referee to protect the interests of the weaker party.[4] Equally, the presumption of contact, particularly in cases of domestic violence, has been

---

[1]   Notably the 'non-intervention principle' of the Children Act, s.1(5) and Schedule 12, para. 31 of the Family Law Act 1996 together with the emphasis on information meetings and mediation to facilitate parental decision-making.

[2]   Bailey-Harris, Barron and Pearce, *From utility to rights? The presumption of contact in practice* (1999) 13 International Journal of Law, Policy and the Family 111.

[3]   Section 11(4)(c).

[4]   Smart and Neale, *Arguments against virtue: must contact be enforced?* (1997) 27 Family Law 332.

strongly questioned, although recent leading cases indicate a move towards a more cautious approach.[5]

The evidence that parents have absorbed these legal messages is mixed. The numbers of applications for s.8 orders, including contact orders, has risen steadily since the implementation of the Children Act in 1991 provoking Pearce et al. to comment:[6]

> Whilst judicial oversight of uncontested arrangements for children has indeed become more attenuated, parents appear to have compensated for this fact by positively forcing themselves upon the courts' attention through the presentation of an ever-increasing number of disputes.

Yet there are also indications that a substantially larger, but unknown, proportion of parents do indeed make their own arrangements for contact without making applications for orders. In 2000, for example, there were only 54,832 applications for contact orders compared to 136,410 divorce decrees absolute granted.[7]

The private ordering principles and contact presumption are therefore contested and there are also indications that family practices are not wholly congruent with legislators' intentions. In this paper therefore I wish to explore what the law, and legal system, does have to offer families making contact arrangements. Drawing on a recently completed study of contact decision-making, I will examine two questions:

1. How pertinent is the law and the legal system in the making of contact arrangements?
2. What are the consequences of engagement and non-engagement with the law in making contact?

---

[5]   *Re L, V, M and H (Contact: domestic violence)* [2000] 2 F.L.R. 334. See also *supra*, note 2 and Kaganas and Day Sclater, *Contact and Domestic Violence – the Winds of Change?* (2000) 30 Family Law 630.

[6]   Pearce, Davis and Barron, *Love in a Cold Climate – Section 8 Applications under the Children Act 1989* (1999) 29 Family Law 22.

[7]   *Judicial Statistics 2000.* Of course, applications for contact orders can arise at any time rather than only during divorce proceedings. However the juxtaposition of the two figures does indicate that the pool of applicants for contact orders is smaller than the pool of divorcing parents, and considerably smaller if former cohabitees are included.

The Contact Project

The Contact Project was a two year qualitative study funded by the Joseph Rowntree Foundation.[8] The study aimed to examine how contact was negotiated and experienced by individual family members (children, mothers and fathers). Sixty one 'families' were recruited into the sample. A third of these were family sets (of mother, father and at least one child), a third consisted of a parental or parent-child dyad and in a third of 'families' a single adult was interviewed. Families were recruited from a wide range of sources, including a court service mailout to petitioners/respondents.

One of the aims of the study was to attempt to identify what gives rise to (or precludes) contact disputes and therefore the sampling strategy was geared to generating a sample roughly divided between disputed and non-disputed cases. It must be stressed that the sample is a purposive not a representative one, that is the aim was to sample a range of cases of different types, including over-sampling 'difficult' or contested contact to facilitate comparison between 'working' and 'not working' contact. Consistent with our aims, the sample, (see Table 1) included a range of levels of involvement with the legal system, ranging from nil or minimal engagement regarding contact through to those where the court had been involved in decision making.

Table 1: Levels of engagement with the legal system regarding contact

Highest level of involvement[9]	Number of families	Percentage
Court welfare report	13	21.3
In court mediation/agreement on court premises or out of court mediation	9	14.8
Solicitors letters re contact	4	6.6
Specific contact advice	5	8.2
General divorce advice	24	39.3
No legal contact	6	.8
Total	61	100

---

[8] Trinder, Beek and Connolly, *Making Contact* (2002) Joseph Rowntree Foundation.

[9] Few interviewees were clear about the precise details of the legal process. The 'court welfare report' category included some who appeared to have had a full hearing. The 'in court mediation etc.' grouping had not had a welfare report ordered, nor had there been a final hearing.

Before considering the relative 'effectiveness' of the legal and non-legal route in establishing contact, I first want to examine the extent to which law and the legal system informs privately ordered contact decision-making.

Shadow bargaining and contact

In a highly influential paper published in 1979 Mnookin and Kornhauser argued that despite the move towards private ordering, the role of law continued to provide 'a framework within which divorcing couples can themselves determine their postdissolution rights and responsibilities'.[10] Their theoretical model of divorce bargaining in the shadow of the law consisted of five factors:

- Parental preferences;
- Bargaining endowments created by legal rules, that is knowledge of the outcome that a court would impose if no agreement were reached;
- Degree of uncertainty about legal rules linked to parental attitudes to risk;
- Transaction costs entailed in going to court and parties ability to bear them;
- The parties' disposition to engage in strategic behaviour.

In order for Mnookin and Kornhauser's model to work parents need to be aware of what their 'bargaining endowments' are. The model posits solicitors as performing a number of functions, including acting as a 'source of information'.[11]

> Lawyers can provide the basic information about each spouse's bargaining endowment – the applicable legal norms and the probable outcome in court if the case is litigated. Indeed, as noted earlier, imprecision in the applicable legal standards increases one's need for legal advice. A rational client will want an accurate assessment of the possible costs of alternative modes of dispute settlement. Lawyers are also an important source of information about transaction costs, a major element of which will be legal fees.

However the evidence from our sample is that the legal shadow cast is targeted rather than universal, and indeed for many it consists of messages to promote private ordering rather than information about bargaining endowments. For some sets of parents (6 in our sample) a strategy of active avoidance of solicitors was adopted. Some of these were cohabitees who did not need to see a solicitor to secure a divorce and had agreed contact arrangements, and some were separated

---

10 Mnookin & Kornhauser, *Bargaining in the Shadow of the Law: The Case of Divorce* (1979) 88 Yale Law Journal 950.

11 Additionally as counselor, clerk, negotiator and litigator: Ibid., at pp. 985-6.

couples with no immediate plans to initiate a divorce. Neither grouping sought advice about contact arrangements and actively defended against 'encroachment' on what were seen as family matters. In 24 cases (the 'general divorce advice' group) at least one, but generally both, parents consulted a solicitor to make arrangements for the divorce. What is remarkable, and pertinent to our discussion of shadow bargaining endowments, is the absence of any transmission of legal rules concerning contact from solicitors to parents, or of any expectation from parents that they should seek or might need legal advice, in any form, from solicitors regarding contact arrangements.

In some cases it appears that the content of these consultations centred on the divorce process and financial settlement and parents could not recall any discussion of contact or residence:

> *It never came up with the solicitor, I don't think we even got that far. It never went to court about the children, so we had no court order on them. [Ex-husband] didn't have a solicitor, so I drove the divorce, my solicitor just wrote to him directly.* Resident mother

Alternatively if contact was discussed, the message given by solicitors was to encourage or support any contact arrangement that parents had devised, though without apparent comment on the nature of the arrangements. The message from solicitors was clearly one of praise for parents who were able to devise their own arrangements, together with the comment that solicitor involvement in contact was likely to be costly as well as potentially conflict-inducing:

> *I went to a solicitors and she was very good, we went through everything, you know, discussed everything and really the bottom line from her was, ... she felt that the way to continue, if the lines of communication are open, to keep that going and if we can come up with an agreement between ourselves, that that's the best way to go, rather than get the solicitors involved right at the beginning, because she said that's really when the shit hits the fan.* Resident mother

> *We've done well when it's concerned to [child], everything's been sorted out just between the both of us. Even the solicitor said that, that it's good to see you can sort it out...getting exactly sorted out what you want and where you go.* Contact father

It was interesting to note that quite a few parents had a perception that the involvement of lawyers could promote rather than avoid disputes:[12]

---

[12]   However, in only one case, of a highly amicable divorce, were the lawyers perceived to act in a non-conciliatory way, though exclusively over financial matters.

I thought I say, I don't want any lawyers involved because we are working out this fine and if we go to a lawyer we are probably going to end up fighting like hell for everything and so we haven't done anything, nothing, we haven't seen anybody its just been us getting on and working things out. Resident mother

In contrast, there appears to be a greater willingness to elicit and proffer legal advice about financial matters:[13]

I had to see a solicitor because of the financial mess he'd left us in, but we decided between us the evening he left what contact he wanted and I was quite happy. Resident mother

[The solicitor] just went with me. She didn't advise for or against, she just went with what I wanted...I didn't think that wasn't an issue, no...the house was an issue, but she did say did I want to stay in the house and I said yes. Resident mother

For 30 out of our 61 cases, therefore, solicitors were either not consulted about contact or were consulted only about divorce proceedings and financial matters, but not contact. In these cases the shadow of the law consisted only of an encouragement to privately order contact rather than information gleaned from a solicitor about how a court might order contact.

We did though find some support for Mnookin and Kornhauser's model. In five of our 61 cases parents had a specific problem with contact and had explicitly sought advice from a solicitor. Here, but only here, was there evidence of private bargaining in the shadow of the law about contact arrangements.[14] For these families what was sought was clarification of their legal position and potential remedies, and for some, an independent view of what were 'appropriate' contact arrangements. The specific issues covered were diverse, including overseas issues (relocation and holidays), stepmother contact, unreliable contact and the frequency of contact.

The advice or information that was given in these 'specific contact issues' cases was remembered[15] and quite clearly matches Mnookin and Kornhauser's model of shadow bargaining where legal rules are transmitted to parents via solicitors. For example in a case possibly involving the residential parent's relocation/extended holiday both parents had sought legal advice and the trip had subsequently been abandoned:

---

[13] Although even here some parents were reluctant to involve solicitors.
[14] No further legal action had been taken at point of the interview although in all cases parents were given clear and specific advice about their legal position and potential remedies.
[15] This provides some reassurance that the lack of advice recalled by other interviewees was not simply due to forgetfulness but rather was a result of their perception that contact was not a (legal) problem.

There'd be no point, because I wouldn't win. I know I wouldn't win. The courts would see it that [father] wasn't going to be having his regular contact with [child] and they wouldn't let him go I don't think. Especially not from having such close contact to having practically nothing all. So my solicitor has told me that she doesn't think I would win if I, you know, if I was going to do something like that. Resident mother

In another case the resident parent had sought legal advice about the divorce in general and also raised the question of the contact arrangements that she felt were unsuitable. What the solicitor had suggested instead was what was essentially the local court practice of a 'standard package'.[16]

But the solicitor had said that what was suitable access was probably one night in the week and every other weekend and he [ex-partner] said 'What a load of rubbish, the solicitor doesn't know what he's talking about.' So it's going to be difficult, even if the solicitor said, 'Look this isn't right', he'll dispute it.... Access arrangements are going to have to be sorted out. And someone might look at it and say whether it's reasonable or not. Resident mother

In contrast her former partner had not seen a solicitor and it was clear that although the informal nature of the arrangements created a sense of insecurity, the 'standard package' local practice transmitted via the solicitor represented a somewhat threatening legal shadow:

Interviewer: *So did you have any advice about separating, did you go to a solicitor?*
I didn't. [Former partner] did, because she did actually start divorce proceedings, but his reaction was that the father should see the children once a fortnight, which keeps coming up sometimes (pause). I'm not sure that the way we've done it is possibly the right way, we did it this way to try and be as amicable as possible. Once solicitors start becoming involved then you're talking about a lot of money, but at the end of the day, I wonder if it is best to get everything settled and written down so that everybody knows where they are. There are probably 'fors' and 'against' for both. I feel I've probably got less control over the children than [mother] has because she's the mum and although they probably spend almost as much time with me as they do with her. I just feel that legally everything is weighted in her favour. That's just the way it is.
Interviewer: *And in that sense if it was drawn up it would be easier. You would feel less vulnerable?*
I would possibly feel less vulnerable, but maybe that would then give me even less access and control than I've got now, I don't know. Contact father

---

[16]   In contrast to the bewildering array of arrangements developed privately, the local court appeared to start from a presumption of a 'standard package' of fortnightly weekend staying contact and a weekday evening.

It is clear from the 'specific contact issues' cases that solicitors can and do operate as the sources of information transmitting legal rules to parents envisaged by Mnookin and Kornhauser, and that these do inform parental decision-making to some degree. However it also appears that this is not an automatic or universal response but is triggered only if contact is presented to solicitors as a problem that one or both parents cannot live with. If parents are relatively satisfied with their contact arrangements their presumption is that contact is a private matter and they do not expect solicitors to inform them about legal rules about contact or to comment on the nature of the contact arrangements. We did not find any cases of parents in these groups who *had* anticipated being advised about contact or who were surprised or disappointed by the private ordering message. The shadow of the law in these relatively low problem contact cases is therefore barely detectable, with both potential transmitters and receivers of legal rules declining to accept the role, unless or until contact was presented and framed as a legal problem.

Our data only comes from parents and children, and we did not interview solicitors. However our finding that it is parents who largely set the agenda about whether or not legal advice about contact is required is mirrored by the recent study of solicitor's practice by Eekelaar et al.[17]

Two other overseas studies have also found that the shadow of the law fades somewhat when put to the empirical test. In a US study of divorce bargaining, Jacob[18] concluded similarly that the shadow of the law does not form a universal backdrop, and that again it is how the issue is presented to solicitors, as problem or non-problem, that determines whether or not legal rules are sought and elicited. A recent study by Dewar and Parker[19] of the new Part VII of the Australian Family Law Act 1975 also characterises the shadow of the law as partial, in particular for litigants in person who had taken themselves out of 'reception range' for the transmission of legal rules. John Dewar[20] has argued further that family law is becoming increasingly fragmented, with a shift from a horizontal 'top-down' model of family law where legislators and judges send out authoritative legal meanings down through the system, to a more horizontal system where there are multiple sites of legal interpretation developed by all the actors in the system, operating within multiple legal shadows and, 'Instead of a single shadow cast by law, as Mnookin and Kornhauser presupposed, there are instead many shadows, with no single shadow covering the whole system'.[21]

---

17   Eekelaar, Maclean and Beinart, *Family Lawyers* (2000) Oxford: Hart Publishing.
18   Jacob, *The elusive shadow of the law* (1992) 26 Law & Society Review 565.
19   Dewar and Parker *Parenting, planning and partnership: The impact of the new Part VII of the Family Law Act 1975* Family Law Research Unit Working Paper No.3 (Griffiths University, 1999) at footnote 106.
20   Dewar, *Family law and its discontents* (2000) 14 International Journal of Law, Policy and the Family 59.
21   Ibid., at p.77.

If the shadow of the law is not universal what does inform parental decision-making in privately-ordered cases? In our sample parents who had privately ordered contact constantly referenced child welfare principles, particularly ideas about putting children first, the importance of ongoing contact, ongoing parental responsibility and of parental amicability:

> *Well I really do think the cliché of not using your children as part of your armoury whatever may have happened between the two of you, they don't deserve any of it and if you do have to split up it needs to be as good as you can make it for them. I don't think you should use them as a weapon either in terms of money or access if you can possibly avoid it because it is important for them.* Resident mother

Although these ideas are highly consistent with the Children Act 1989 they were not expressed as legal principles. Instead it appeared that these core welfare principles relate to widely-circulating social norms drawing upon, as do legal principles, a body of social science research and policy.[22]

The role of law, in many cases, is therefore minimal, even non-existent with many families operating contact arrangements out of reception range of the shadow of the law but underpinned by common child welfare principles. This level of private ordering was, in fact, precisely what the architects of the Children Act 1989 had wished to encourage as much as possible, and it has clearly been given further impetus by the support of solicitors to parents who have reached their own agreements. Nonetheless some commentators might consider that the level of private ordering beyond any reach of the shadow of the law is a cause for concern. In the next section I will consider whether or not these concerns are justified.

The effectiveness of private ordering and court-based processes

The nature of contact arrangements and the process of decision-making varied widely across the sample. The 61 families were classified into the following three groups:[23]

1. *Consensual committed:* both parents and children were committed to regular contact and interparental conflict was low or suppressed (27 families).
2. *Faltering:* contact was irregular or had ceased without court involvement. No regular contact had ever been established or adhered

---

[22]   See also Jacob, *supra* note 18.
[23]   For a full account of the three umbrella groups and their nine sub-types see Trinder, Beek and Connolly, *Making Contact* (2002) Joseph Rowntree Foundation.

to and both parents were, or had become, ambivalent about the value
of contact (8 families).

3. *Conflicted:* role conflicts and/or perceptions of risk resulted in disputes
   about the amount or form of contact (26 families).

The levels of engagement with lawyers and courts were equally divergent with half
of the families in the sample with entirely privately ordered arrangements, whilst
the other half of the sample had had much more substantial engagement with the
legal system at various levels, ranging from exchanges of solicitors' letters through
to final hearings. In this section I want to explore the consequences or outcomes of
engagement or non-engagement with the law/courts. It does however make little
sense to compare directly the efficacy of the private ordering versus the legal/court
solution. The two halves of the sample were not internally homogeneous but in
overall terms the private ordering and court route groups did differ significantly in
the degree of difficulties they were experiencing over contact. The court route
families were generally facing significant and often long-standing contact
problems, whereas the private ordering families in comparison had relatively minor
difficulties with contact from the beginning. A more useful question then is to ask
whether the right families were proceeding down the right route, and whether each
route offered a workable solution for its particular constituency.

Defining 'workable' or 'good enough' is, of course, extremely difficult. The
definition we derived from the data is as follows:

Working or 'good enough' contact requires that *all* the following apply:

- Contact occurs without risk of physical or psychological harm to any
  party;
- All parties (both adults and children) are committed to contact;
- All parties are broadly satisfied with the current set of arrangements
  for contact and do not seek significant changes;
- Contact is, on balance, a positive experience for all parties.

Not working or 'not good enough' contact is defined as when *at least one*
of the following applies:

- Contact poses an ongoing risk of physical or psychological harm to at
  least one party;
- Not all parties are committed to contact;
- At least one party seeks significant changes to the existing contact
  arrangements;
- That contact is, on balance, not a positive experience for all parties.

On these definitions the 'consensual committed' arrangements were classified as working, whilst the faltering and conflicted arrangements were classified as not working.

Table 2: The relationship between contact grouping and legal involvement

	Private ordered (no legal contact, general divorce advice, specific legal advice)	Legal contact (solicitors letters, in/out of court mediation, welfare report)
Working Contact: Consensual committed	25	2
Not Working Contact: Faltering Conflicted	5 5	3 21

Is private ordering good enough?

The majority of private orderers fell into the umbrella group of 'consensual committed' arrangements. These were arrangements characterised by high commitment of both parents to contact. Some families were characterised by frequent contact and friendly relationships between parents:

> Interviewer: *Do you speak to dad on the phone?*
> *Yeah loads of times. Same with Mum when I go round to Dad's. They are friends but they don't want to live with each other because they have rows.* Child (7-9 age band).

In some families parental relationships were equally warm, but practical problems of time and distance meant that contact was less regular. Both parents worked together to get around these barriers:

> *We always meet. Again we've got a good agreement there. We meet at ..... It's roughly about half-way for both of us.* Contact father

In other families there was regular ongoing contact with both parents supportive of each other's relationship with the children despite a degree of parental tension, often stemming from the separation:

> *Everybody has said to me, 'Oh I think you're being remarkable', you know, but I have to think about them, I have to put them first and I just think that if we were*

shouting and screaming at each other, it just doesn't get you anywhere. Resident mother

Although adults and children in all of the 27 'consensual committed' families were positive overall about contact, it is vital to recognise that these types of arrangements were not without difficulties. What made contact work in this grouping was an implicit role bargain where contact parents accepted their non-resident status, and in turn, resident parents proactively facilitated contact. This bargain in itself was challenging. For resident parents the degree of proactive facilitation of contact by residential parents necessitated a considerable and continuing engagement with the non-residential parent who may not be behaving entirely as the residential parent might wish. This 'children first burden' came at a personal emotional cost:

> *I mean in the beginning, it was very much about territorial, you know, over the children, but it's not like that, because we are adults, we know each other very well and at the end of the day, he's still their father and no matter what he's done to me, I try not to let that cloud the issue, I try not to influence, well, I try not to influence them.... I don't like what he's done at all and I'm very hurt about it all, but I wouldn't necessarily know how to use it really, because I don't think I'd want to, because ultimately it will hurt them.* Resident mother

Equally for non-resident parents acceptance of their role could result in a significant sense of loss of role as a parent, and an insecurity about their position and relationship to the children:

> *I think earlier on there was a sense of relief somehow. I think I would get a little keyed up before I saw them, even feel a bit nervous at the time and then when I saw them it was like a terrific sense of relief, you know I kind of grabbed them and hugged them like never before and you know, that kind of thing as if...so pleased that we were still part of a unit somehow. I think as the years have gone by I've changed in that I'm a little more secure...* Contact father

Despite these difficulties all parties remained committed to contact and contact proceeded relatively smoothly. Both parents recognised the other parent's parenting ability and there was some level of shared decision-making. There was no current physical or psychological risk or perception of risk to adults or children although incidents of domestic violence may have occurred in the past, particularly around the time of the separation. Both parents, but especially the residential mothers articulated currently dominant child welfare discourses consistent with, but not referencing, the Children Act 1989, in particular ideas about putting children first, enduring parenting (and therefore contact) post-separation, the right and need of children to have contact and the importance of avoiding interparental conflict. Contact arrangements were made by parents, with some checking out with children. Legal involvement in contact issues was minimal with the highest level of involvement being the early exchange of solicitors' letters in two cases before contact settled down.

The example of the 27 'consensually committed' families does suggest that the private ordering option can and does work extremely well, facilitating the development of arrangements that are sensitive to the needs of each party and flexible enough to respond to changes in family circumstances and children's changing needs and wishes. In this respect therefore the non-interventionist thrust of the Children Act 1989 appears to be working well, enabling parents who have the capacity to do so to make workable contact arrangements without external intervention that are consistent with the child welfare principles of the Act.

However, not all of the privately ordered arrangements were working as well. Five of the 26 conflicted cases and five of the eight faltering arrangements were privately ordered. The five conflicted privately ordered cases were all part of the 'competitively enmeshed' sub-type where contact was generally frequent but changeable, accompanied by a sense that parents were locked in ongoing competition for the children, played out through contact arrangements. Although the principle of contact was not disputed, the pattern of contact was a major ongoing source of parental tension, although never escalating into outright conflict. Both parents in these cases felt that the other had more control over arrangements Resident parents were not seeking to end contact, but instead turn what were seen as chaotic and burdensome arrangements for the children (and themselves) into a 'standard package' of weekly or fortnightly weekend contact, with themselves clearly established as the residential parent:

> *My vision of when your mum and dad separate is that your dad comes and takes you out on a Sunday and you go the zoo. But it is control, control.* Resident mother

In turn contact parents did not accept a clearly secondary parenting role, felt that the resident parent was undermining their relationship with the children and sought to maintain or increase contact:

> *I felt that unfair pressures had been put upon the children, not to spend as much time with me as they wanted ... there always has been a lot of pressure in that direction, according to the children.* Contact father

Children were aware of the hostility and competition between parents and often altered arrangements to move towards more 'equal' arrangements in an attempt to manage the conflict. In several cases legal advice had been sought but no applications for contact orders had been made, ostensibly to avoid either the cost of legal action or a legal battle:

> *Once solicitors start becoming involved then you're talking about a lot of money, but at the end of the day, I wonder if it is best to get everything settled and written*

down so that everybody knows where they are. There are probably 'fors' and 'against' for both. Contact father

I think at that stage, neither of us, he or I wanted a solicitor's battle and I think he had heard a lot of stories about how, by the time the two solicitors have finished with you, you really hate each other. Resident mother

Five of the faltering cases were also privately ordered. In three of these cases the resident parent had accepted that contact was not going to occur, or occur regularly, and was not taking any steps to secure a contact timetable. For the two resident parents who still wanted to establish a contact regime the decision not to seek mediation or contact orders was based on a perception that the legal system would or could do nothing to enforce contact:

[Solicitor] suggested two things. She said getting a private detective to find out a bit more about his circumstances because being in [city] I've very little way of knowing what exactly is going on. And secondly, this court action to enforce contact, but I didn't really want...I didn't think that going, as I say, enforcing contact through a court would be particularly helpful to the relationship. Resident mother

Although contact and private ordering was not working in these conflicted and faltering cases the option remained of taking legal action. The question then arises as to whether or not further legal advice or legal involvement, or equally advice or support from another quarter, would have improved the situation. We turn now to what happened in those cases where more extensive use was made of the law.

Does the law provide good enough solutions?

The contact problems experienced by those who went further up the legal ladder than specific legal advice were generally of a significantly higher order than for the private ordered cases. Finding a good enough outcome therefore was likely to be much more challenging. The critical question however was whether or not the law, at all its levels, could produce a workable settlement, or even more importantly a resolution of the problem.

Of the half of the sample that made more extensive use of the law to tackle contact issues, the issues involved largely centred around three types of problems:

- *Faltering contact cases:* where the residential parent wanted to establish contact, or more contact on a reliable basis, against the apparent wishes of the non-residential parent;
- *Risky contact cases:* cases where the residential parent perceived themselves and/or the well-being of the child(ren) to be at risk due to

risk of domestic violence, physical sexual or emotional abuse of the child, neglect or abduction;

- *Role conflict cases:* where the non-residential parent was seeking to establish contact, or more contact, against the apparent wishes of the residential parent and/or child(ren).

Role conflict cases

Eleven of the cases in the sample involved high and sometimes prolonged levels of conflict or acrimony between the parents where the non-residential parents were seeking more contact against the wishes of the residential parents (and possibly the children). What was striking from our data was the limited capacity of the law or courts to facilitate damaged parental relationships. In some of these cases court involvement was followed by no contact when the 'defeated' parent dropped/was pushed out of contact; alternatively a contact regime could be established but with no parental communication or a series of ever more tightly defined orders could continue to fuel conflict and lead to further entrenched positions. For these couples it is clear that having one's day in court does not clear the air but provides a further source of conflict, sometimes erupting into violence scenes.[24] Residential and non-residential parents were united however in their dissatisfaction with the legal system. In each of these cases the parents were highly distressed and preoccupied by the battle and the continuing sense of persecution by the other parent, but also the children were deeply distressed, acknowledged by the parents but blamed on the other's actions:

> *I've gone up the school and they've said 'He's been in tears all day, because "something about the judge", sobbing uncontrollably'. So I managed to actually speak to her [mother] and ask her 'What are you doing, why are you doing it?' ... the last weekend I had him he said ... 'The judge, Dad, I'm going to have a word with him', he said, 'It should be half each'. So, I don't know where he's getting it from. I've been taking all the Welfare Reports very seriously and, but he's been involved so much he knows exactly what's going on.* Contact father

> *The poor kids are standing there and we just get in the car..., I said 'I'm sorry you had to witness that' [assault between new partners] and Annie just goes 'why can't you talk, why can't you talk' and that's all she was. Chris said nothing at all.... That's him you see, he is very sensitive and he just doesn't show any emotion whatsoever. He just never cries.* Contact father, ongoing battling

---

24   Including reports of a residential stepfather assault on non-residential stepmother, non-residential stepmother assault on non-residential father and assault by police on non-residential father following harassment of residential mother.

In some cases the children had resolved the conflict by rejecting the non-residential parent and wishing he were dead:

> *I would never ever ever ever ever have contact. I would say for my bit I wish [father] died.* Child [5-7 age band]

This was a small sample and there are clearly cases outside of our sample where legal involvement is facilitative. However the difficulty the courts have with handling high conflict cases has long been recognised. Buchanan et al.'s study[25] of a sample of 100 families who have been through the welfare reporting system reaches somewhat similar conclusions, with a majority of parents critical about the court process and finding the process highly stressful. Only a quarter of parents were completely satisfied with contact arrangements 12 months on. As worrying was the high and continuing levels of distress experienced by both children and adults at the end of the legal proceedings and one year on. In their study of contact applications Pearce[26] et al. conclude that 'We are inclined to conclude that what the legal process offers in response to children applications is: (a) psychological containment; and (b) a mechanism through which parents can express their hurt and grievances. It does not offer an effective means of determining behaviour in the longer term'. The evidence from our study and that of Buchanan et al. would suggest that this is an overly benign view of the process and that court involvement in these high conflict cases does not contain but is iatrogenic, inflaming parents' sense of hurt and grievance, together with a worrying degree of spillover of conflict to children.

Risky contact cases

Considerable attention has been given recently to the potential of contact as a source of harm to mothers and children after separation or divorce. In ten families the primary issue about contact from the point of separation was the attempt to continue contact whilst attempting to manage potential risk to a parent or child from domestic violence, physical, sexual or emotional abuse of the child, neglect or abduction. These were cases where the conflict related to managing risk rather than disputes clearly about the relative involvement of each parent in the child's life. None of the resident parents were seeking to terminate contact although all were seeking continuing or further safeguards.

In none of the supported contact cases were residential parents explicitly seeking to terminate contact, although for one residential mother it was contingent upon the

---

[25] A. Buchanan, J. Hunt, H. Bretherton, & V. Bream, (2001) *Families in Conflict: The Family Court Welfare Service: the perspectives of children and parents.* Bristol: The Policy Press.

[26] *Supra.* note 6, at p. 27.

child's continuing desire to see the non-residential parent. With the exception of an indirect contact only case, the highest level of vigilance in these cases was a supported contact centre. Contact parents were frustrated at having to use the centre and wanted unsupported contact. Residential parents expressed some concern or disquiet about the level of security or supervision offered by supported contact centres:[27]

> *I don't leave [child] in there with him.*
> Interviewer: *You stay?*
> *Yeah I wouldn't leave [child] alone with him.... As soon as I walk out of there I am always watching over my shoulder in case he is following me.* Resident mother

We could not make any assessment about whether or not contact was safe in these cases. What does emerge is that there are few options to ensure that contact can be made completely safe where resident parents and children are wanting contact to occur. The resident parents had all found their lawyers supportive. However it was clear that the level of security offered by supported contact centres is not commensurate always with the residential parent's perception of risk.

Faltering contact cases

In three of the eight faltering cases the resident parent took action to attempt to establish a contact regime, initiating an exchange of solicitors' letters or going to mediation. As the resident parents in the privately ordered faltering group had suspected, the capacity of the system to ensure contact was extremely limited. In none of the three cases did these interventions lead to any alteration in the contact arrangements:

> *She has been good, but she said at the end of the day other than, you know, forcing him in a car and bringing him here every week what more? - I have got to go and see her again and say well can we turn it the other way, where do I stand if I say fine, right, I will give him another month, if he doesn't do it regularly for a month can I then turn round and say 'fine that's it, I have been pushed far enough' you know.* Resident mother

Conclusion – the limits of law

Dewar and Parker argue that a pattern of 'bifurcation' has emerged in Australia following the introduction of the Family Law Reform Act 1995:

---

[27]   See also C. Furniss, *The process of referral to a family contact centre: policies and practices* (2000) 12 C.F.L.Q. 255-281.

... the legislation seems to have intensified the pre-existing dispositions of parents
– that is, those parents who were in any case inclined to agree now have a much
richer range of resources with which to frame that agreement, while those parents
who were in any case inclined to disagree now have a much more powerful
armoury with which to do so. As a Registrar put it, 'the legislation is good for
people with good intentions and bad for those with bad intentions'. [28]

A similar pattern is evident in England and Wales with a large group of parents
taking advantage of the Children Act 1989 to establish their own contact
arrangements, whilst a significant group of parents either drop out of contact or
experience conflicts over roles or safety.

John Dewar[29] is, however, ambivalent about the consequences of privatisation.
His positive reading is that the law is facilitating private choice and being
responsive to individual difference. However his negative reading is that the state
is withdrawing from its perceived roles of guaranteeing fairness of outcomes or
redressing inequalities in bargaining power.

The suggestion from our study is that the negative reading is somewhat alarmist.
From our data it appeared that in general, although not always, private ordering
does work and works well largely outside of the shadow of the law, with parents
attempting to 'do the right thing' drawing heavily on the same social norms about
contact that also underpin the Children Act 1989. Equally our study suggests that
the assumption that private ordering disempowers either men, or women or
children in the search for parental agreement is overly simplistic with more
complex distributions of power in evidence. In the privately ordered cases where
contact was working a gender and generational power balance had been struck
where residential parents undertook to facilitate contact and non-residential parent
undertook to commit to contact but not to challenge the role of the residential
parent. Contact did not work where this power balance was unstable or contested,
where residential parents did not actively facilitate contact and/or where non-
residential parents challenged the residential parent's power and status or physical
security. In the privately ordered groupings there were no obvious instances of
younger children being sat down and having their wishes and feelings ascertained.
What did occur though was a general checking out with younger children by
parents acting as authoritative but not authoritarian parents, and a willingness to
allow teenagers to take control of arrangements. In contrast the children in the
conflicted and faltering groupings appeared disempowered.

On this basis I would argue that the no order principle and privatisation thrust of
the Act has worked surprisingly well although these are not typically the families
that come to the attention of many researchers, practitioners or policy-makers.
What the law does offer for these therefore is a set of messages supporting contact

---

[28]   *Supra*, note 19 at p.80.
[29]   *Supra*, note 20.

but enabling families to make their own arrangements, with the possibility of the law as a fallback when things are not working.

However when contact relationships are not working the capacity of the law to mend them is inherently limited. Michael King[30] quite rightly, in my view, refers to the 'inherent impotence' of the courts in regulating and controlling human relationships, a view echoed recently by Thorpe L.J. in fading contact and high conflict cases.[31] Law can improve things, certainly in our specific contact issues cases, legal advice proved helpful in some cases and there will be many instances of cases outside of our sample where the framework provided by the courts proves helpful. However it also clear from our sample that we cannot expect the law or courts to do much to assist fading contact cases where neither party is especially committed to contact (even though the children might be). Equally it is clear that continued legal involvement in high conflict cases is destructive rather than constructive and expensive in emotional and financial terms for the participants. There is a vital role for the law in risky contact cases; however the remedies available are not necessarily sufficient to guarantee safety.

The law does have things to offer to children and parents who face difficulties in organising contact. Perhaps its greatest contribution is to offer families the possibility of making contact arrangements that meet their individual circumstances. The evidence from this study is that a substantial, but unknown, proportion of families will do this well, although not without difficulties. Equally solicitors have a role to play in offering advice about contact where parents present contact as a problem. Beyond that the law should provide a protective role where contact involves risk to one or more participants; it can also act as an arbiter of last resort. Where contact is problematic however, the law by itself can do little to repair parental trust, co-operation and compromise that are critical for working contact. We need a wider range of solutions to be available, including mediation and supported and supervised contact services. We also need more advice and ideas about conflict-resolution strategies to be made available for parents. Above all we need a range of therapeutic services, similar to programmes developed in the USA that address relationship issues[32] rather than simply imposing a solution without addressing the underlying issues.

---

[30] King, *Playing the Symbols - Custody and the Law Commission*, (1987) 17 Family Law 186-91.

[31] See *Re L, V, M and H (Contact: domestic violence)* [2000] 2 F.L.R. 334.

[32] See, for example, J. Johnston, & L. Campbell, *Impasses of Divorce: The Dynamics and Resolution of Family Conflict* (1988). New York, Free Press; H. McIsaac, & C. Finn, *Parents beyond conflict: a cognitive restructuring model for high-conflict families in divorce. Family and Conciliation Courts Review*, (1999) 37, at p.74; N. Thoennes, & J. Pearson, *Parent education in the domestic relations court: a multisite assessment.* (1999) Family and Conciliation Courts Review, 37, at p.195.

Chapter 3

Cross-frontier Contact between Children and their Parents: Identifying the Problems

William Duncan

This chapter identifies some of the challenges in achieving a more effective international system for securing the child's right to maintain contact with both parents when they live in different countries. The text is drawn from a more extensive report of the Hague Conference on Private International Law which has been drawn up by the author, entitled *Transfrontier Access/Contact and the Hague Convention of 25 October 1980 on the Civil Aspects of International Child Abduction* – Final Report (July 2002).[1]

The dynamics of the problem

The issue of contact will usually arise in the context of the breakdown of the marriage or other relationship of the parents. In the international context the parents will often have different national origins. The question of contact may have to be considered in the light of other problems arising from the breakdown. The custodial parent may, for example, be applying to a court for permission to relocate to another country (usually his/her country of origin);[2] this would be more likely to happen in a common law than a civil law jurisdiction. One parent may have abducted or unlawfully retained the child, or be alleged to have done so, in another jurisdiction.[3] There may be allegations of violence or abuse either in respect of the child or the other parent. The circumstances of the parents following the breakdown of the marriage or other relationship are often subject to rapid and

---

[1] These extracts chosen reflect the subject matter of the seminar which was given by the author at the University of East Anglia.

[2] As, for example, where a mother applies to a court for permission to take a child out of the jurisdiction against the objections of a father whose rights (by operation of law or by court order) include a veto on removal of the child.

[3] In civil law countries, such as Germany or Austria, applications for relocation are rare because the custodial parent generally has the right, as an incident of custody, to move with the child to another country.

unexpected changes.

It may be helpful to begin with a brief description of some of the typical fact situations giving rise to difficulties over the exercise of contact in transfrontier context.

(a)   In the context of applications for the return of a child under the *Hague Convention of 25 October 1980 on the Civil Aspects of International Child Abduction*, the applicant may wish to establish contact with the child pending the decision on return. It has been suggested that in a case where delay occurs in determining the return application, denial of contact with the applicant parent may contribute to the alienation of the child from that parent, and may thereby increase the prospects of an Article 13 *b)* defence succeeding. In any event, preserving the continuity of the child's relationship with the applicant parent requires that the issue of contact be dealt with as quickly as possible.

(b)   When a return application is refused, *e.g.* on the basis of an Article 13 defence, the question immediately arises of the appropriate arrangements for contact between the child and the left behind parent.

(c)   There are those cases where a parent from abroad applies, outside the context of an abduction, for the enforcement of a contact order made in another jurisdiction. A typical case is where a court of the country where the child had his or her previous habitual residence permits the parent who is the primary carer to relocate to another jurisdiction together with the child, but at the same time makes a contact order with respect to the left-behind parent. There is a connection between this type of case and the phenomenon of abduction. If no respect is given abroad to contact orders made in the context of relocation orders, this may affect the willingness of judges to permit relocation, where such permission is required; and, if judges are unwilling to allow relocation, this may precipitate abductions by primary carers.

(d)   There are cases where a parent from abroad applies *de novo* for a contact order from the authorities of the State where the child lives. The importance of facilitating the application derives principally from the interest which the child has in maintaining beneficial links with both parents. In addition, as the framers of the 1980 Convention recognised, the failure to support a reasonable application for contact by a non-custodial parent may itself fuel the temptation to abduct.

(e)   There are cases where modification of existing cross-frontier contact arrangements is sought either by the custodial parent or the parent exercising contact. These cases may range from modification sought in order to restrict or even terminate the exercise of contact, to those cases where changes in circumstances are thought to require practical adjustments to contact arrangements.

(f)   There are cases where the custodial or non-custodial parent claims that transfrontier contact terms have been breached, and seeks an order to restore the *status quo*. The extreme case is unlawful retention where, following a period of transfrontier visitation, the non-custodial parent refuses to return the child. The alleged infringement may be less dramatic. The parent exercising contact may unilaterally decide to alter some of the terms on which contact was agreed/ordered, for example, by extending the period of contact unilaterally or by not providing details of the child's movements as had been agreed. Equally the custodial parent may place obstacles in the way of agreed contact, as for example, by not allowing agreed telephone access, by not passing on correspondence, etc.

(g)   There are cases where access is about to occur – *e.g.* the child is about to travel to spend a school holiday with the non-custodial parent, or the non-custodial parent is about to travel a long distance to visit the child – and the custodial parent at the last minute raises objections, based perhaps on fear that access terms will be breached. The non-custodial parent may in such a case need to have his/her application dealt with on an emergency basis if access is to go ahead as arranged.

In the above examples, the terms 'custodial' and 'non-custodial' parent are used. The cases may of course be more complicated where this distinction does not readily apply, for example, in some cases of joint custody where there may be an initial problem of determining whether the rights in question are access rights or rights of custody. The 1980 Hague Convention itself, in Article 5, defines rights of custody as including not only 'rights relating to the care of the person of the child', but also 'the right to determine the child's place of residence'.[4]

Some fundamental principles

The right of the child to maintain personal relationships with both parents, even when the parents live in different States, is now an almost universally accepted norm.[5] Among other relevant principles, which appear in international instruments are the following:

(a)   The right of the child who is capable of forming his or her own views to express those views freely, those views to be given due weight in accordance with the age and maturity of the child.[6]

(b)   The right of all family members to have their family relationships respected by the law.[7]

---

[4]   Article 5.

[5]   See Article 10(2) of the *United Nations Convention on the Rights of the Child* (adopted and opened for signature, ratification and accession by General Assembly resolution 44/25 of 20 November 1989. Entered into force on 2 September 1990, in accordance with Article 49) [hereinafter the 'CRC']. The CRC has 181 State Parties.

[6]   Ibid., Article 12(1).

[7]   See, for example, Article 8 of the *European Convention for the Protection of Human Rights and Fundamental Freedoms* (opened for signature by the Council of Europe on 4 November 1959; entered into force on 3 September 1953), and the judgments of the European Court of Human Rights, *infra*, at note 35. See also

(c)   The right of the child to protection in the case of dissolution of the parents' marriage.[8]

(d)   The right of all persons, especially children, to be protected from physical or other abuse.[9]

(e)   The common responsibility of men and women in the upbringing and development of their children, it being understood that the interest of the children is the primordial consideration in all cases.[10]

Some general objectives for the international framework

By way of preface, it should be stressed that at the national level, the problems surrounding contact, in the absence of agreement between the persons involved, are difficult to resolve, subject to differing approaches in domestic laws, and often give rise to chronic litigation. The difficulties are multiplied at the international level by the geographic distance, as well as legal, linguistic and other cultural differences between the countries concerned. One cannot expect to achieve at the international level more than is achievable within national systems.

The law can be a somewhat blunt instrument when applied to the maintenance of long-term human relationships. In the area of parent/child contact, one of its principal functions is to provide a framework, which will encourage and support agreed solutions. Unless parents can achieve a minimum level of co-operation, disputes on the terms of contact tend to occur time and time again and may result in costly and ineffective litigation. This introduces another preliminary consideration, that of cost. The provision of services, whether they be judicial or administrative, to assist in resolving frequently occurring transfrontier contact disputes can be extremely costly.

While the law cannot itself guarantee the successful development of long-term human relationships, such as those between parents and children, it should be capable of providing a firm legal framework which:

---

[8]   Article 10 of the *International Covenant on Economic, Social and Cultural Rights* (adopted and opened for signature, ratification, and accession by United Nations General Assembly resolution 2200 A (XXI) of 16 December 1966. Entered into force on 3 January 1976, in accordance with Article 27).

        Article 23(4) of the *International Covenant on Civil and Political Rights* (adopted and opened for signature, ratification and accession by United Nations General Assembly resolution 2200 A (XXI) of 16 December 1966. Entered into force on 23 March 1976, in accordance with Article 49).

[9]   See Article 19 of the CRC, *supra* note 5.

[10]   Article 5b of the *Convention on the Elimination of All Forms of Discrimination against Women* (adopted and opened for signature, ratification, and accession by United Nations General Assembly resolution 34/180 of 18 December 1979. Entered into force on 3 September 1981, in accordance with Article 27(1)).

(a)   promotes agreement between parents concerning access/contact arrangements and supports agreements once made;

(b)   discourages vexatious or repetitive litigation concerning access/contact;

(c)   provides a secure legal background against which the custodial parent may feel safe in releasing a child for access/contact, *i.e.* with a degree of confidence that the conditions of contact will be adhered to and that the child will be returned after a period of visiting contact is complete;

(d)   provides a framework within which the non-custodial parent may with confidence expect access/contact arrangements to be respected by the custodial parent;

(e)   deters conduct by either parent designed to frustrate the enjoyment of access/contact or to break the conditions of access/contact;

(f)   offers reasonable assistance to foreign parents seeking to effect access/contact in an unfamiliar legal system; and

(g)   offers reasonable facilities for supervised access/contact, or other appropriate protective measures, where unsupervised access/contact is not in the best interests of the child.

An integrated approach

The sections which follow identify and survey the different elements which impact on the resolution of international access/contact disputes. The elements surveyed are diverse. They cover both the concerns of private international law (questions of international jurisdiction, recognition and enforcement and co-operation between authorities in different countries), as well as aspects of national law including matters of substance, procedure and enforcement. The overall picture needs to be explained and understood if attempts to improve the system are to be effective. Most of the elements are interrelated. Reform of isolated parts of the system without regard to the context carries a risk of failure. For example, improvements in the international system for the recognition and enforcement of decisions on access/contact will be undermined if national enforcement procedures are ineffective. Domestic procedures and rules of substance need to be reviewed in terms of their impact on international cases. Improvements in the facilities and services provided to foreign applicants, and in the access which they are given to foreign legal systems, may count for little if the procedures adopted and the substantive rules applied to their cases are insensitive to the special features, including the problems arising from time, distance and language, which are peculiar to international cases.

The importance of agreed jurisdictional standards

It has been suggested that, while the law itself cannot guarantee the successful development of relations between children and their parents who are in different countries, it should nevertheless be capable of offering a firm legal framework within which agreement is encouraged, unnecessary conflict and litigation is avoided, contact arrangements are secure and unjustified obstructions to contact are deterred. An essential element in this stable legal framework is a set of agreed standards for exercising jurisdiction to make or modify contact orders in cross frontier situations, as well as provisions for the recognition and enforcement of contact orders made on the basis of those agreed standards. A coherent and universal set of jurisdictional standards is essential for three reasons:

(a)   To avoid conflicts of jurisdiction when applications for contact are first considered. Where there exists the possibility of the authorities/courts of more than one country exercising jurisdiction, the danger exists of duplicated litigation, with attendant costs and the generation of inconsistent orders. Even if duplication is avoided by a 'first come first serve' (*lis pendens*), this may still be an incentive for a parent to seize rapidly the more convenient forum, an outcome which is in conflict with the principle that parents should be encouraged to settle their differences concerning their children by agreement and without litigation if possible.

(b)   To ensure that jurisdiction exists to make contact orders when this is in the interests of the child. Existing gaps, *e.g.* where jurisdiction to make interim orders is absent, need to be filled.

(c)   To circumscribe jurisdiction to modify an existing contact order. If an existing contact order may too readily be modified by the authorities in a country in which the child has a temporary residence, especially where that residence occurs for the purpose of exercising contact in that country, a situation of uncertainty is created which encourages litigation, promotes conflicting orders, places in jeopardy existing and possibly agreed contact arrangements and acts as a strong disincentive to courts when considering whether to give permission for the exercise of contact abroad.[11] At the same time, it is important to have realistic but closely circumscribed jurisdictional principles, which enable the terms and conditions of contact to be modified in situations of emergency, even by the authorities of a country in which a child is merely present.

In summary, it may be said that the international picture with regard to jurisdiction to make or modify contact orders has up to now been a rather unsatisfactory one.

---

[11]   It is this consideration which inspires Article 15 of the Council of Europe draft *Convention on Contact Concerning Children.* "Article 15 – Conditions for implementing transfrontier contact orders: The judicial authority of the State Party in which a transfrontier contact order made in another State Party is to be implemented may, when recognising or declaring enforceable such contact order or at any later time, fix or adapt the conditions for its implementation, as well as any safeguards or guarantees attaching to it, if necessary for facilitating the exercise of this contact, provided that the essential elements of the order are respected and taking into account, in particular, a change of circumstances and the arrangements made by the persons concerned. In no circumstances may the foreign decision be reviewed as to its substance."

There has been a great deal of uncertainty on many issues, as well as the potential for competing jurisdictions. It was against this background that negotiations began in 1994 at The Hague for what was to become the *Hague Convention of 19 October 1996 on Jurisdiction, Applicable Law, Recognition, Enforcement and Co-operation in respect of Parental Responsibility and Measures for the Protection of Children.*

Assistance to foreign applicants

A foreign applicant, seeking to enforce an existing contact order or applying for a contact order *de novo*, whether or not under the umbrella of the 1980 Convention, faces a range of difficulties over and above those confronting an applicant in a purely domestic case. The difficulties arise from distance, from lack of familiarity with language, legal system and other relevant services, and from the probable absence of any personal or familial support network in the foreign country. Without appropriate support, the struggle by an applicant to obtain transfrontier contact can be very costly and often proves to be overwhelming. The issue therefore arises of the level of services which it is possible or appropriate for the authorities in the requested State to make available, bearing in mind that those services are provided not only for the benefit of the applicant but also in the interests of the child or children concerned. Some of the specific issues that arise are as follows:

(a) What information should be provided (and in what languages)?
(b) What legal advice should be made available?
(c) What degree of assistance in accessing the legal system is appropriate and in particular should there be some level of free legal aid or assistance?
(d) What facility should exist to promote an agreed outcome?
(e) What supports should be provided for contact arrangements which are agreed or ordered, *e.g.* to facilitate supervised contact or to assist with travel arrangements for the child?

Recognition and enforcement of foreign contact orders

The recognition and enforcement of contact orders which have been made on a substantial jurisdictional basis is an important element in achieving some order within the international system. The absence of recognition principles may lead to re-litigation, to disadvantages for the left-behind or non-custodial parent, and it may act as a disincentive when a court is considering an application by the custodial parent for relocation. However, there are a very broad range of different circumstances that need to be taken into account in considering appropriate recognition and enforcement procedures and standards. On the one hand there is the relatively simple case where the court of the child's habitual residence has made a relocation order combined with contact provisions, and the custodial parent, immediately following relocation, refuses to comply with the access conditions.[12] Here there is a strong case for a simple and speedy procedure for recognition and enforcement. Contrast this with a case in which the contact order was made several years ago by the authorities of the State in which the child had a former habitual residence. Assume that the contact provisions have worked reasonably well in the meantime and have been somewhat modified over time by agreement between the parents. However, circumstances have changed; the child has grown older and has begun to form his or her own views. A dispute then arises which the parents are unable to resolve, as in the past, by agreement. The issues here relating to enforcement of the original contact order are far more complicated. The swift and unreflective enforcement of an ageing contact order may be inappropriate. There may be good reasons not to enforce the original order or at least to allow some modification of it, particularly where the requested State is the jurisdiction in which the child now has his or her established home. Cases of this kind point to the need for a careful balance between the principle of automatic recognition and questions concerning jurisdiction to modify a contact order. Put another way, it is important that recognition principles should be underpinned by clear and coherent jurisdictional standards. This is the philosophy underlying the *Hague Convention of 19 October 1996 on Jurisdiction, Applicable Law, Recognition, Enforcement and Co-operation in respect of Parental Responsibility and Measures for the Protection of Children.*

'Chapter IV [of the 1996 Convention] supplies a detailed set of rules which were lacking in the 1961 Convention for the recognition and enforcement in a Contacting State of measures of protection taken in another Contracting State.'[13] Orders relating to access/contact made by an authority exercising jurisdiction under the Convention are entitled to be recognised by operation of law in all other Contracting States.[14] The grounds for refusing recognition are narrowly drawn,[15] and the recognising State is bound by the findings of fact on which jurisdiction was based in the State of origin.[16] Provision is made for advance determination of whether access/contact orders made in one State may or may not be recognised in another State.[17] Enforcement of access/contact orders in the State addressed takes place, in accordance with the procedure provided for in the law of that State,[18] as if those measures had been taken by the authorities of that State and to the extent provided by its law.[19] The procedure by which the order is declared enforceable or

---

[12] See e.g., the New Zealand case *Gumbrell v. Jones* [2001] N.Z.F.L.R. 593.

[13] See the Explanatory Report of the *Convention of 19 October 1996 on Jurisdiction, Applicable Law, Recognition, Enforcement and Co-operation in respect of Parental Responsibility and Measures for the Protection of Children*, P. Lagarde, Actes et Documents of the XVIII Session, Volume III, 1998, 534-605, available at http://www.hcch.net/e/conventions/exp134e at paragraph 20.

[14] Article 23(1).

[15] Article 23(2).

[16] Article 25.

[17] Article 24.

[18] Article 26(1).

[19] Article 28.

registered for enforcement must be simple and rapid.[20]

Unlawful retention

The primary remedy provided by the 1980 Convention – the return order – provides strong support for access/contact arrangements. The wrongful retention of a child in breach of custody rights is placed on the same level as wrongful removal of the child.[21] An order for the return of the child 'forthwith' applies.[22] The Convention thus contains the primary sanction against the most serious abuse of rights of access/contact across international frontiers, namely the unlawful retention of the child following a period of agreed or court ordered access. At the same time the existence of this sanction supports the child's right of contact by creating a situation in which a custodial parent or a court may feel more secure in agreeing to or approving arrangements for overseas contact with the non-custodial parent. The order for return in the case of unlawful retention is subject to the same carefully balanced defences as apply to unlawful removal.

When the provisions of the 1980 Convention are combined with those of the 1996 Convention, the position of the custodial parent is further strengthened in a case of unlawful retention. The 1996 Convention confirms the primary jurisdiction enjoyed by the authorities of the child's habitual residence,[23] and Article 7 ensures that in a case where a child has been unlawfully retained following a period of access in another jurisdiction, the authorities in the country where the retention has occurred will not acquire general jurisdiction, even if they have refused to return the child,[24] until a number of strict conditions are satisfied. Until these conditions are met, the authorities of the habitual residence will retain jurisdiction and any order made by them will be entitled to recognition[25] and enforcement.[26] 'The combined effect of the two Conventions is to make it completely clear that wrongful behaviour should not be rewarded, and that the best interests of the child are served by following the [1980] Convention's mandate and returning the child. Non-return is the last resort, not the acceptable alternative.'[27]

Promoting agreement and mediation

Arrangements concerning contact which are agreed between the parties have

---

[20]   Article 26(2).
[21]   Article 1.
[22]   Under Article 12.
[23]   See Article 5.
[24]   For example under Article 13 of the 1980 Convention.
[25]   Article 23.
[26]   Article 28.
[27]   Gloria F. de Hart, *The Relationship between the 1980 Child Abduction Convention and the 1996 Protection Convention* (2000) 33 New York Jo. of International Law and Politics 94.

several advantages over arrangements which are ordered by a court. They are more likely to be adhered to by the parties; they establish a less conflictual framework for the exercise of contact and are therefore strongly in the interests of the child; and once a certain level of co-operation between the parents is established, the painful and expensive pattern of re-applications to the court for orders for modification or enforcement is less likely to become established.

The need to promote agreed solutions was recognised by the framers of the 1980 Convention, which in Article 7, paragraph 2c) requires Central Authorities to take all appropriate measures to secure the voluntary return of the child or to bring about an amicable resolution of the issues. In practice, in contact cases under the 1980 Convention, most Central Authorities try to achieve an agreed settlement as a first step (the survey of applications which were made in 1999 shows that 20% of applications under the 1980 Convention were resolved by voluntary agreement). This will typically involve at least a letter to the custodial parent, and may sometimes involve attempts to negotiate an amicable settlement. However, the precise supports given to the negotiating process differ from country to country. In a few jurisdictions, mandatory mediation applies to contact disputes, as well as to other family law cases. In some other States, mediation services are available though not mandatory. Mediation may be in-court or out-of-court. In a small minority of jurisdictions, conciliation/mediation services are provided free of charge. There is little evidence of mediation facilities which have been developed with the special requirements of international cases in mind. The services of the International Social Service may sometimes be invoked.

The patchwork nature of the supports available to promote agreement in international contact cases is not surprising, and reflects the fact that domestic systems are at different stages of development, particularly with regard to the provision of mediation services. Whether the special requirements of promoting agreement in international cases would benefit from additional provisions within international instruments is a matter for discussion. The Hague Convention of 1996 contains a provision which is more explicit than that of the Hague Convention of 1980, but which still leaves much to the discretion of States Parties. Article 31 b) mandates Central Authorities, directly or indirectly, to 'take appropriate steps ... to facilitate, by mediation, conciliation or similar means, agreed solutions ... in situations to which the Convention applies'.[28]

An important initiative was the establishment in December 1998 of the Franco-German Mediation Commission,[29] consisting of three Members of Parliament from each of the two States, appointed by the respective Ministers of Justice. The Commission has mediated in a number of difficult disputes involving French and

---

[28] The proposed European Council Regulation on parental responsibility also gives Central Authorities a role in promoting agreement through mediation or other means. Brussels, 3.5.2002, COM(2002) 222 final.

[29] The establishment of the Commission was agreed between the Ministers of Justice of France and Germany at a Franco-German summit meeting in Potsdam, Germany. See the Joint Report of the French and German Parliamentary members of the Franco-German Mediation Commission, 2 May 2002.

German parents, with the objective of restoring personal relations between the two parents concerned and their children. The Joint Report of the Commission, published in May 2002, indicates that most of the 41 cases referred to the Commission have involved disputes over access/contact and in 9 of these cases the Commission was able to organise, or was on the point of organising, access for the applicant parent. In a further 4 cases a similar outcome appeared possible, and there are 8 files currently under consideration. Once the parents have agreed to undergo mediation, two members of the Commission, one from France and one from Germany, are assigned to the case. It is possible for the mediators to propose the use of experts, in particular psychologists. The work of the Members of the Commission has been personally time consuming, but their successes have led them to raise the possibility of putting in place a professional mediation system to deal with transfrontier cases which might work under their authority.

The mediation project which the UK non-governmental organisation 'Reunite' is about to embark on is worth noting. It is directed particularly towards those cases where a return order is sought primarily for the purpose of securing rights of access. The typical case is where the abductor is the primary carer of the child, and (usually) the father is relying on his joint rights of custody to apply for a return order, not so much because he wishes to have custody transferred to him, but because he views the return application as the best available means of preserving contact with his child. Cases of this sort seem to be an appropriate target for mediation in that for both parties there are strong incentives to reach agreement over the terms of access. The mother may be able to avoid the return order; the father for his part may be able to achieve his real wishes without the costs and delays involved in further litigation in his home country. Quite apart from this, the project may help in a more general way to identify the main issues which need to be addressed in developing an effective system of international mediation.[30]

National laws and procedures

It is as well to be aware of differences in the approaches of domestic systems to the substantive issues surrounding contact, and of the possible impact of these differences on the possibilities for international co-operation. Certain fundamental principles are subscribed to by almost all States. Under Article 9, paragraph 3 of the *UN Convention on the Rights of the Child*:[31]

> States Parties shall respect the right of the child who is separated from one or both parents to maintain personal relations and direct contact with both parents on a regular basis, except if it is contrary to the child's best interests.

---

[30]   See Anne-Marie Hutchinson, *Mediation in International Child Abduction Cases*, a paper presented to the 2001 World Congress on *Family Law and the Rights of Children and Youth*, Bath, England, 19-22 September 2001.

[31]   *Supra.*, note 5.

In addition, under Article 10, paragraph 2:

> A child whose parents reside in different States shall have the right to maintain on a regular basis, save in exceptional circumstances, personal relations and direct contacts with both parents ...

The European Court of Human Rights has asserted on several occasions that the right of contact belongs to the parent as well as the child, and that it is a fundamental right, shared mutually between parent and child, and protected under Article 8 of the European Convention on Human Rights. In its decision in the case of *Elsholz* v. *Germany*[32] the Court stated as follows:

> The mutual enjoyment by parent and child of each other's company constitutes a fundamental element of family life, even if the relationship between the parents has broken down, and domestic measures hindering such enjoyment amount to an interference with the right protected by Article 8 of the Convention.

The rights enjoyed under Article 8 are not absolute and each State has a margin of appreciation in deciding whether limits, within the meaning of Article 8, paragraph 2 of the European Convention on Human Rights, are 'necessary in a democratic society', *e.g.* to protect 'the health and morals' or 'the rights and freedoms' of the child. However, strict scrutiny is required in respect of restrictions on parental rights of access.[33] The Court has recognised that unreasonable restrictions on visiting rights may lead to the increased alienation of a child from his or her parent.[34] The basis for this approach is Article 8 of the European Convention on Human Rights and the case law developed under it by the European Court of Human Rights, including the principle that the State has a positive obligation, inherent in an effective respect for family life, to maintain and develop family ties.[35] The idea of 'necessity' when applied to restrictions on contact implies the further principles that there should be no other less restrictive method available of protecting the interests of the child and that the restrictions should be proportionate.

The first objective of the Council of Europe draft Convention on Contact concerning Children is 'to determine general principles to be applied to contact orders'.[36] These principles are to be implemented in the internal laws of States Parties and are to be applied by the judicial authorities. The intention is that the adoption of common standards should also facilitate co-operation and the mutual

---

[32] Judgment of 13 July 2000, citing inter alia *Johansen v. Norway*, Judgment of 7 August 1996 and *Bronda v. Italy*, Judgment of 19 June 1998.

[33] Ibid.

[34] See for example, *Kutzner v. Germany*, Judgment of 26 February 2002.

[35] See *Airey v. Ireland* (1979), Series A, No.32; *Marckx v. Belgium* (1979), Series A, No.31; *Kroon and others v. Netherlands* (1994), Series A, No.297c; *Keegan v. Ireland* (1994) 18 E.H.R.R. 342.

[36] Article 1(a).

recognition of contact decisions at the international level.[37] Article 4 affirms the right of the child and both his or her parents to maintain regular contact. Contact may be restricted or excluded only where necessary in the best interests of the child.

Despite the broad acceptance of certain fundamental principles, it is clear that the application in practice of these fundamental principles varies in different countries. There are differences with respect to the focus of access/contact rights. Is the focus the parent, the child, or both? There are differences in the definition of the class of persons entitled to claim or exercise access/contact rights.[38] There are differences in the starting points from which access determinations are made; some systems accept a more or less strong presumption in favour of access/contact between the child and the non-custodial parent, while others regard the interests of the child as the primary or paramount consideration. These differences become more apparent and pronounced when issues of child abuse or domestic violence are involved. In several countries the development of an appropriate approach to access/contact in cases where there has been a history of domestic violence has been a subject of debate for a number of years.[39]

There are other differences in the substantive rules applied to access/contact cases, which are more specifically related to international situations. There are, for example, some jurisdictions where the judicial practice is not to allow the child to travel abroad to enjoy a period of contact with the non-custodial parent in the latter's country of residence.[40] Sometimes also, the conditions attached to access are restrictive, particularly in a case where there is a risk of abduction. Our consultations have revealed some concerns that the conditions imposed on access do not always take into account the special difficulties experienced by parents who have to travel long distances to enjoy access. The principle enjoined by the European Court of Human Rights, that restrictions on access should be no more

---

[37]   See the Preamble to the Convention and the Explanatory Report on the Convention at paragraph 10.

[38]   Article 4 of the Council of Europe draft *Convention on Contact with Children*, which is based on the jurisprudence of the European Court of Human Rights, allows persons other than parents having 'family ties' (e.g. close family relations or persons having a *de facto* family relationship with the child) with a child the right to apply for contact with that child. See *Scozzari and Giunta v. Italy* (2000), Series A, paragraph 221 and *Boyle v. United Kingdom* (1994), Series A, No.282/B.

[39]   See e.g. the Advisory Board on Family Law: Children Act Sub-Committee (England and Wales), *A Report to the Lord Chancellor on the Question of Parental Contact: Cases where there is Domestic Violence*, Lord Chancellor's Department, Spring 2000, and the decision of the Court of Appeal in *Re L, V, M and H (Contact: Domestic Violence)* [2000] 2 F.L.R. 334. For a recent comment on the debate, particularly in Australia, see Helen Rhoades, *The 'No Contact Mother': Reconstructions of Motherhood in the Era of the New Father* (2002) 16 I.J.L.P & F. 71; see also Family Law Council (Australia), *Child Contact Orders: Enforcement and Penalties*, June 1998. In New Zealand there is now a presumption against contact where domestic violence is established.

[40]   For example, Chile.

than necessary to achieve their objective (usually the safety of the child) appears not always to be respected in practice.

Procedural obstacles and inadequacy can often present the most serious threat to the effective exercise of rights of access/contact. It is significant that the European Court of Human Rights has in a series of cases decided over recent years paid particular attention to this issue, and has in a number of decisions found breaches of Article 8 of the European Convention on Human Rights arising from the decision-making processes in certain European States. In particular, the Court has held that the applicant parent must be able to be involved in the decision-making process sufficiently to provide him or her with the requisite protection of his or her interests.[41] 'The decision-making process leading to measures of interference must be fair and such as to afford due respect to the interests safeguarded by Article 8.'[42] The Court has also been concerned to ensure that procedures are such that accurate information is obtained concerning the views of the child and the relationship between the child and the applicant parent.[43]

Prior guarantees and safeguards

Measures under national law to help guarantee, in advance, adherence to the terms and conditions of contact orders are of great importance. They may be particularly helpful when the child is to travel to another jurisdiction for the exercise of contact with the non-custodial parent. They are also useful when the child is to relocate to another jurisdiction with the custodial parent to ensure that the custodial parent abides by the terms and conditions of any contact order. Guarantees and safeguards

---

[41] See *Elsholz v. Germany*, *supra* note 32. In the *Elsholz* case the combination of a refusal to order an independent psychological report and the absence of a hearing before the relevant Court revealed insufficient involvement by the applicant in the decision-making process and led to a breach of both Articles 8 and 6 of the European Convention on Human Rights.

[42] See *Ciliz v. Netherlands*, Judgment of 11 July 2000, in which a failure to co-ordinate the decision-making processes: (a) involving the applicant's expulsion from the country concerned, (b) concerning access to his child, constituted a breach of Article 8.

[43] In *Sahin v. Germany*, Judgment of 11 October 2001, the failure of the relevant Court to obtain correct and complete information on the child's relationship with the applicant parent (including a failure to hear the child) revealed that the applicant was not sufficiently involved in the access proceedings. The Court should not have been satisfied with an expert's vague statements about the risks inherent in questioning the child. There was a breach of Article 8. See also *Sommerfeld v. Germany*, Judgment of 11 October 2001, in which the Court affirmed that correct and complete information on the child's relationship with the applicant parent was an indispensable prerequisite for establishing a child's true wishes and thereby striking a fair balance between the interests at stake. In the circumstances, hearing the child without having available psychological expert evidence in order to evaluate the child's seemingly firm wishes was not satisfactory on the part of the deciding Court.

are part, along with firm provision to deal with unlawful retention, of the legal background against which the custodial parent may feel safe in releasing a child for contact. Though it is appropriate to recall, where prior guarantees and safeguards constitute restrictions on the exercise of access/contact, that such restrictions should be proportionate in the sense of not going beyond what is necessary to secure the protection and well being of the child. Prior guarantees and safeguards may also be ordered for the benefit of the party exercising access to help to ensure that the custodial parent does not block the access rights of the non-custodial parent. They are, in this context part of the 'framework within which the non-custodial parent may with confidence expect contact arrangements to be respected by the custodial parent'.

One of the objectives of the Council of Europe Convention on contact concerning children is to establish appropriate safeguards and guarantees for both national and international cases to ensure the proper exercise of contact and to ensure the return of the child at the end of a period of contact.[44] A non-exhaustive list of safeguards and guarantees is set out in Article 10, paragraph 2, and States are obliged to provide under their laws for at least three categories of safeguards and guarantees. The safeguards to ensure that a contact order is carried into effect include supervised contact, the obligation of a person (either the parent seeking contact or the person with whom the child lives, or both) to provide for travelling and accommodation expenses for the child, the deposit of a security to ensure that contact is not frustrated, or the imposition of a fine.[45] Safeguards to ensure that the child is not improperly removed or retained when contact occurs include the surrender of passports or identity documents, the provision of financial guarantees, and charges on property.[46] Other safeguards or guarantees mentioned are undertakings (*i.e.* specific promises or assurances given to a court by a litigant), a requirement that the person having contact report regularly to a competent body, the issuing of a certificate in the country in which contact is to take place recognising in advance the custody or residence order in favour of the parent with whom the child usually lives, an advance declaration of enforceability of the contact order in that State, and restrictions as to the place where contact is to be exercised.

Enforcement under national law

Neither the automatic recognition of contact orders, nor indeed their enforcement 'without any special procedure being required',[47] can guarantee a uniform approach to, or a uniform standard of, enforcement. The reason for this is that it is the national law of the State where enforcement is to take place, which will be

---

[44]   Article 1.b.
[45]   Article 10(2)(a).
[46]   Article 10(2)(b).
[47]   See Article 46 [Rights of Access] of the Proposal for a Council Regulation on parental responsibility, *supra* note 28.

likely, finally, to determine what methods of enforcement are available, and on what conditions and according to what procedures and time frame they may be applied. For example, the Hague Convention of 1996 provides that enforcement should take place 'in accordance with the law of the requested State to the extent provided by such law, taking into consideration the best interests of the child'.[48]

The approach to enforcement of contact orders under national law differs markedly from one country to another. The most important differences lie perhaps in the processes of enforcement and their time frames, rather than in the precise sanctions, which may ultimately be applied for breach of a contact order. In some States, for example, non-compliance is met first with attempts at mediation; in others, by contrast, even a risk of non-compliance may result in a detailed court order. Opposition by the child to the contact arrangements produces different consequences in different States. In some, the opposition of a child may render enforcement impossible; in others, it may give rise to attempts to mediate. Rights of appeal against an enforcement order differ. In general, there are important differences in the opportunities afforded to the custodial parent to delay enforcement and, therefore, there are often considerable differences in the period of time that elapses between breach of a contact order and the application of a sanction. There is no doubt that the problems in this area constitute one of the major causes of friction, frustration, expense and complaint on the part of parents who are trying to maintain contact with their children across international borders. On the other hand, efforts are being made in several countries to improve the situation.[49]

---

[48] Article 28. Article 50 of the proposed Council Regulation on parental responsibility provides similarly that 'the enforcement procedure is governed by the law of the Member State of enforcement'.

[49] In this context, it is interesting to note that the German Federal Supreme Court, in a decision of 19 June 2002, awarded damages to a father entitled to have contact with his child, because the custodial mother had not complied with the terms of the contact order. The significance of the judgment in general terms goes beyond the individual case because the court clearly states that, where there is a contact order specifying details on how contact is to take place, it is not for the custodial parents to replace the court's considerations of the child's best interests by his or her own (Bundesgerichtshof [Federal Supreme Court], 19 June 2002 – XII ZR 173/00). Also of interest is a Resolution (No.3) on the general approach and means of achieving effective enforcement of judicial decision, of the Ministers participating in the 24th Conference of European Ministers of Justice (Moscow, October 2001). The Resolution invites the Committee of Ministers of the Council of Europe to instruct the European Committee on Legal Co-operation (CDCJ) to identify common standards and principles at a European level for the enforcement of court decisions.

Summary

The principal shortcomings in the international system for securing cross-frontier rights of access/contact may be summarised as falling in the following broad areas:

(1)   The failure to have in place uniform rules determining the jurisdiction in international cases of authorities to make or modify contact orders and adequate provisions for the recognition and enforcement of foreign access/contact orders.

(2)   The absence of agreement among States on the nature and level of the supports which should be made available to persons seeking to establish or secure access/contact rights in a foreign country. This refers *inter alia* to information and advice, including legal advice, assistance in gaining access to the legal system, facilities to promote agreed outcomes, and the physical or financial supports, which are sometimes necessary to enable access/contact which has been agreed or ordered to take place.

(3)   The operation in some countries of procedures, both at the pre-trial and enforcement stages, which are not sufficiently sensitive to the special features and needs of international cases, and which are the cause of unnecessary delays and expense.

(4)   An inadequate level of international co-operation at both the administrative and judicial levels.

For further discussion of possible strategies to overcome these problems, the reader is invited to read the final chapter of the Hague Conference on Private International Law, *Final Report on Transfrontier Access/Contact* (July 2002) drawn up by the author.

Chapter 4

Recent Developments and Problems in Scottish Children's Law

Alastair Bissett-Johnson*

Constitutional divisions in family law-devolution and human rights

Whilst readers from federal jurisdictions will not be surprised to find that aspects of family law are divided between state or provincial and federal law,[1] the impact of the different consequences between breach of human rights law by the Westminster Parliament (in reserved matters) and the Scottish Parliament (in devolved matters[2]) is one novel consequence of the Scotland Act 1998.[3] Most family law in Scotland is within the jurisdiction of the Scottish Parliament. Nevertheless, there are certain noteworthy exceptions such as social security, child support, aided conception and abortion, which are reserved to Westminster.[4] One obvious difference between the

---

[*] With acknowledgment to my colleagues Fiona Raitt and David Brand for their assistance with earlier drafts of this paper and to my research student Lucia Polanski, LL.B. (Hons), D.L.P.

[1] As with the distinction in Canadian law between divorce and ancillary matters which are Federal and property division which is Provincial. See P. W. Hogg *Constitutional Law of Canada*, Carswell (2000). A similar distinction is found in Australian law between Federal and State law see F. Finlay, R. Bailey-Harris and M. Otlowski, *Family Law in Australia* (5th ed.) Butterworths, Australia (1997).

[2] E.g. most of the rest of family law, though the practice has emerged of the Scottish Parliament deferring to Westminster under the so-called 'Sewel motions' in matters of family law where a U.K. wide approach to a problem in family law such as international adoption is desirable. The Children and Adoption Bill 2002 provides an example of this. The First Minister, Jack McConnell, in the Official Report (of the Scottish Parliament) for April 4, 2001 Col. 1191 stated that a U.K. wide approach was needed in respect of (i) intra-country adoption orders, (ii) further restrictions (including catching those on the internet) were required to prevent advertising of inter-country adoptions and (iii) tighter restrictions were required on persons wishing to bring a child into the U.K. for the purpose of adoption. A further Sewel motion in October 2001 aimed at ensuring a Scottish input into the U.K. list of designated countries whose orders would automatically be recognised in the U.K.

[3] For more detail on the Scotland Act see A. C. Page, C. Reid and A. Ross, *A Guide to the Scotland Act 1998*, Butterworths (1999) and on Human Rights Law in Scotland see R. Reed and J. A. Murdoch, *A Guide to Human Rights Law in Scotland*, Butterworths, Edinburgh (2002).

[4] See the list of specific reservations in Sch.5 Part II. For a more detailed discussion of

effect of breach by the Parliament at Holyrood from that of a breach at Westminster is the ability of the Scottish courts to strike down incompatible Scottish legislation[5] rather than merely making a declaration of incompatibility as would be the case of offending Westminster legislation.[6]

It is necessary to make a further distinction in the case of devolved family law antedating the European Convention on Human Rights. If the basis of the infringement is Westminster legislation, then the Scottish courts will grant a declaration of incompatibility, following which the Secretary of State may direct the Scottish Executive to take action under s.58(2) of the Scotland Act, 1998. For example, the appropriate member of the Executive may secure passage of devolved legislation to ensure compliance with the Convention. On the other hand, where the breach of the Convention is due to a pre-existing provision of Scottish common law, then the Scottish courts can strike down the provision.

Whilst the Human Rights Act is not primarily concerned with the family, certain rights that are given status as law under the Act do affect family law matters. Most notable are Article 3, the prohibition on cruel or inhuman treatment,[7] Article 6(1) which provides a right 'to a fair hearing by an independent and impartial tribunal', and Article 8 which guarantees every person 'respect to privacy in their family life'. A problem lies in the fact that rights and freedoms are not absolute. Any interference with family life, such as refusing contact or taking a child into care, may be justified if the interference serves a legitimate state aim that is in proportion to the restriction of the right. In assessing this, States are allowed a margin of appreciation.

Children's capacity[8]

The attitude of Scots law has, at the overt level, probably granted greater autonomy to children than in England. The system of minors and pupils which preceded the Age of Legal Capacity (Scotland) Act 1981 was predicated on the Roman law distinction

---

the Scotland Act see Page, Reid and Ross *A Guide to the Scotland Act 1998*, (Butterworths, Edinburgh, 1999). However even in reserved matters such as child support, the underlying Scottish law may make the Child Support Act 1991 operate differently North and South of the Border. Thus a child at 12 who is habitually resident in Scotland has an independent right to seek a maintenance assessment (s.7 Child Support Act 1991) and a university student can seek child aliment in the courts in his or her own name (see Family Law (Scotland) 1985 s.1(i)(a) and 2(4)(b) under the exception to the jurisdiction of the Child Support Agency created by the Child Support Act 1991 s.8(7)(a) and s.55(i)(b). (In *Macdonald v Macdonald* (1998) Greens F.L.B 31-1 a university Law student sued his mother, a solicitor, for aliment.)

[5] A consequence of the requirement in s.29(2)(d) of the Scotland Act 1998 that the Scottish Parliament must legislate in accordance the European Convention on Human Rights.

[6] Ibid., fn. 3, item 1, ch.8.

[7] See *A v. U.K.* (1999) 27 E.H.R.R.611.

[8] See Edwards and Griffiths, *Family Law*, W. Green, Edinburgh (1997) ch.2 and Sutherland, *Child and Family Law*, T & T. Clark, Edinburgh (1999) ch.3.

between pupils,[9] who generally[10] had no active legal capacity[11] but could be the passive recipient of rights,[12] and minors, who had active capacity to enter into legal transactions provided that they acted with the concurrence of their guardian who was known as a *curator*. The position was both placed on a statutory footing and significantly altered by the Age of Legal Capacity Act, 1991, and further refined by the Children (Scotland) Act 1995.[13]

Section 1 of the 1991 Act sets up a general rule that a Scottish child acquires legal capacity on attaining 16 years and then qualifies it by a series of exceptions in s.2. Section 2 (1)(a) allows a child to enter into legally binding transactions of a kind commonly entered into by persons of his age and circumstances provided that the terms are not unreasonable. Although this would allow quite a young child to buy sweets or soft drinks and older children to buy more expensive items,[14] more difficult questions arise when a child seeks to do a newspaper round or Saturday morning job. This is governed by a combination of the Children (Protection at Work) Legislation 1998 (which amends the Children & Young Persons (Scotland) Act 1937),[15] and local authority bylaws. In 1998, the Scottish Office, Education and Industry Department issued a Circular[16] aimed at implementing Regulation 94/33EC by requiring Local Authority compliance and drew attention to the fact that the EU Regulation required revision of existing bylaws so that 13-year-olds henceforth were not permitted to be employed in jobs not expressly specified in bylaws. Thus express provision would have to be made if 13-year olds were to be able to deliver newspapers or milk or to do light work assisting on the family farm. Attached to the Circular model bylaws for local authorities to consider, though subject to the condition that restrictions on Saturday and holiday working by children were henceforth to be dealt with by the 1937 Act rather than bylaws. The 1937 Act basically ensures in s.28 that, subject to bylaws, children cannot be employed under age 14. They can only do light work;[17] they can not work before 7 on a school day,[18] during school hours or after seven on any day. On school days and Sundays the hours of work are restricted to two hours, and on other days the total work day cannot exceed 8 hours for 15-year-olds and above or 5 hours for those under that age. In addition, children are guaranteed two

9   Defined as girls up to age 12 and boys up to age 14.
10 Though the detailed operation of the rules was complex, see further Edwards and Griffiths, *Family Law* (*supra*) and Sutherland, *Child and Family Law* (*supra*).
11 They generally had to enlist the aid of their guardian (usually a parent) who was called their tutor and who gave the necessary legal consent.
12 Thus they could own or inherit land unlike the position in England under s.1(6) of the Law of Property Act 1925 which precludes a child from owning the legal estate in land.
13 For more detail see E. Sutherland (*supra*) and Edwards and Griffiths (*supra*) ch.3.
14 Sutherland op.cit. gives the example of designer jeans bought at the usual (high) price.
15 See also the Children (Performances) Regs 1968 as amended.
16 3/1998 dated May 28th 1998.
17 Defined in s.2A as involving tasks not harmful to the safety, health or development of children or harmful to their attendance at school or work experience.
18 A number of Dundee law students have adverted to a practice of turning up before 7 to set up their paper round before leaving the news agents at 7. This almost certainly breaches the rules.

weeks a year free from work during school holidays. It is believed that compliance with these rules is, at best, patchy.[19]

The Children (Scotland) Act 1995 added a new s.2(4A) to the Age of Legal Capacity Scotland Act 1981 to ensure that a child with a general understanding of what is involved has power to instruct a solicitor in a civil matter. A child of 12 and above is presumed to have the necessary understanding, but mature children below age 12 may also be able to instruct a solicitor. No leave from the court is necessary. Sutherland[20] suggests that it will normally be for the solicitor approached by the child to make the assessment of the child's understanding even when the solicitor stands to gain financially from the institution of the proceedings since any challenge to the competency of the child to instruct a solicitor would, in practice, be raised by the other party to the proceedings. The reality is that in most cases the power will only be used where the interests of the parent and child conflict. This would include the case where the parent(s) are unwilling to fund the child's litigation but where legal aid might be available.[21]

Although parental rights have long been thought to dwindle as a child approaches majority,[22] readers from outside Scotland may be surprised to learn that Scottish children have capacity to make wills, both of heritage and moveable property,[23] and to consent to adoption (or to veto being adopted) from the age of 12,[24] save where the court is satisfied that the child is incapable of consent when it may dispense with the need for the child's consent.[25] In this latter connection, the paradigm case for court resolution may be step-parent adoption where the court may either find that the child is reluctant to have his legal ties to his paternal family severed by adoption, or where the court feels that the child has been 'coached' by the parent with whom he resides into consenting to the adoption but where the child is incapable of appreciating the long term consequences of the adoption. The first inklings of a decline in step-parent adoption in Scotland to 50% from the 59% of all adoptions which they previously

---

19   See P. Hunter, *The School of Hard Knocks: Employment of Children*, ch.13 in (ed A. Clelland and E. Sutherland, *Children's Rights in Scotland* (2nd. ed.) 2001, Greens. Edinburgh. At para.13.21 Hunter states that 'rarely has so much legislative effort combined to achieve so little practical effect' and cites (*inter alia*) at p. 253 a series of B.B.C. progammes showing Glasgow children working as late as 2 a.m. Perhaps more worrying were the scenes of children selling newspapers late at night by darting in and out of traffic to sell papers to car drivers.

20   op. cit., p.101.

21   See *Airey v Ireland* on the duty of the state to provide legal aid for complex civil cases.

22   See Lord Denning's comments in *Hewar v Bryant* [1970] 1 Q.B. 357.

23   Though it will be rare for a child to have the assets or the desire to exercise this power.

24   This is still older than the age of 7 fixed by the law of Ontario; see Children and Family Services Act R.S.O. 1990 as amended c.C11 Part VII, s.137(6). The Ontario child's rights are, however, tempered by counselling provisions under s.137(7) and a power in the court to dispense with their consent under s.137(9).

25   See s.12 (8) of the Adoption Act (Scotland) as amended by the Children (Scotland) Act 1995.

represented[26] may be relevant to the way the law is now operating. A related problem is of siblings in which an older child is unwilling to be adopted by a step-parent but in which younger children are either willing to be adopted or are too young to have a legal right to consent to the proceedings. For a child to exercise the right in a meaningful way it is crucial for the child to have all the relevant information on which to base his or her choice. It would be unfortunate if a child was only allowed information where adults thought that this was convenient.[27] The advent of s.6 of the Children (Scotland) Act 1995, which instructs parents to take children's wishes into account wherever practicable taking into account the child's age and maturity,[28] reinforces the importance which Scotland attaches to the views of the child and its desire to conform to Article 12 of the U.N. Convention on the Rights of the Child.[29]

Parental responsibility

The Children (Scotland) Act 1995 goes farther than English law in spelling out parental responsibilities and rights (PRR) and one might say that parental rights are bestowed under Scots law largely to enable parents to discharge their legal parental responsibilities. Parental responsibilities and rights are only bestowed on parents who were married[30] to one another at the time of the child's conception or subsequently.[31] Fathers of children born outside marriage have either to acquire PRR by either making an irrevocable[32] agreement, in prescribed form, signed by both parties and registered in the Books of Council and Session,[33] or by making an application to court under s.11 of the Children (Scotland) Act 1995. In both England and Scotland there is evidence of considerable ignorance by unmarried fathers of their lack of rights and it is not

---

26 The current figure of 50% is found in the 2000 Report of the Registrar General for Scotland p.151. In 1997 The Scottish Office Statistical Bulletin, Social Work Series did a detailed breakdown of Adoptions in Scotland p.13, which showed that in 1993 55% of adoptions were step-parent adoptions, a figure which rose to 59% in 1994 before falling back to 56% in 1995.

27 See for instance Sutherland's discussion of C, Petrs 1993 SLT (Sh.Ct) 8 in 1994 SLT (News) 37 where a child was kept in ignorance at the time of his adoption that his biological father was different from the person who he treated as his father and who would become his legal father as a result of the adoption order being made.

28 The same section presumes a child to be competent at 12 though a child may be sufficiently mature at an earlier age. For a discussion of the means of ascertaining children's views see Tisdall, Marshall, Clelland and Plumtree, *Listening to the Views of Children* [2002] J.S.W & F.L 385.

29 For further detail of the Scottish approach to the rights of the child see Cleland and Sutherland, *Children's Rights in Scotland* (2nd ed) (2001), Greens/ Sweet & Maxwell, Edinburgh.

30 Including voidable marriages and void marriages where it was believed by them (whether by error of fact or law) in good faith to be valid. Children (Scotland) Act 1995 s.3(2).

31 Children (Scotland) Act 1995 s.3(1)(b).

32 Save where set aside by the court.

33 s.4 Children (Scotland) Act 1995, the Books of Council & Session are the Public Register in Scotland of official documents.

surprising that in both jurisdictions there have been promises of legislation to confer PRR on at least those fathers who have joined in the birth registration of their children.[34] Where PRR are conferred under the 1995 Act they include the responsibility:

(a)   to safeguard and promote the child's health, development and welfare, and
(b)   to provide in a manner appropriate to the stage of development of the child-
    (i)   direction and
    (ii) guidance to the child.[35]

The responsibility to give guidance to the child ceases at 18 whilst the other responsibilities cease at 16.[36]

The rights which accompany the responsibilities include under s.2(1) of the 1995 Act:

(a)   to have the child living with him or otherwise to regulate the child's residence;
(b)   to control, direct or guide in a manner appropriate to the stage of development of the child, the child's upbringing;
(c)   if the child is not living with him to maintain personal relations and direct contact with the child on a regular basis;[37] and
(d)   to act as the child's legal representative.

The Scottish attitude to the welfare of the child and the extent of the parental responsibilities to control the upbringing of their children and the use of physical correction is possibly different from that in England. The Scottish Law Commission[38] had proposed to forbid parents from using any stick, belt or instrument to cause or risk causing injury to a child or to cause pain or discomfort to the child for other than a short period. At one stage the Scottish Executive had proposed to go further to protect the welfare of children under 3 by forbidding their parents from smacking them on penalty of committing a criminal offence. However, the proposal attracted considerable criticism, despite the comments from the Minister of Justice in *The Scotsman* of March 28 2002, that procuratorial discretion would confine prosecutions to serious assaults. However, when s.51 of the Criminal Justice (Scotland) Act 2003 was passed, the restrictions on corporal punishment were confined to (i) cases of shaking a child, (ii) striking a child on the head or (iii) striking a child with an instrument. Any parental right of physical

---

[34]   In England see *Procedures for the Determination of Paternity and the Law of Parental Responsibility*, L.C.D. March 6, 1998 and in Scotland the White Paper, *Parents and Children*, Scottish Executive (2000) para.2.13.
[35]   Children (Scotland) Act 1995 s.1.
[36]   Ibid., s.1(2).
[37]   Failure to exercise this right may lead to the need for the parent's agreement to the adoption of the child being dispensed with see s.16 of the Adoption (Scotland) Act as amended by Sch.2 of the Children (Scotland) Act 1995.
[38]   See S.L.C. Report 135 on *Family Law* (1992) Recommendation 11, p.33.

correction will be tested against the circumstances in which it took place, the duration and frequency of the correction, its mental and physical effect on the child, the child's age, and characteristics including the sex and state of health of the child. The proposal to abolish the parental right to smack was ultimately rejected as having insufficient support from Members of the Scottish Parliament,[39] despite support for such a ban by children's organisations.

The rights under s.2 can be exercised by each parent without the consent of the other save that, subject to any court order, no person (including a parent) is entitled to remove a child habitually resident in Scotland from the jurisdiction where both parents have PRR without the consent of the other parent.[40]

The PRR are subject to the ostensible duty of parents under s.6 to take the wishes of a child into account as far as practicable and having regard to the age and maturity of the child.

The aspirational character of this provision is exposed by the lack of case law on the section. Assuming that the parents' decision to divorce is a major decision in the child's life it is interesting to examine evidence from England. In England when parents took part in the pilot 'information meetings' held under the Family Law Act 1996, many were unwilling to pass on the pamphlets about parenting plans to their children because they were alleged to be too upsetting for the children or the children were alleged to be too young to understand.[41]

Children's Hearings[42]

After 40 years the Scottish Children's Hearing system is well known for its informal dispositions of cases involving children.[43] The system has become part of the *volksgeist* of the nation.[44] Decisions are made by a panel of locally nominated and recruited, unpaid[45] lay persons,[46] appointed by the Secretary of State. The three person

---

[39] See *The Times* September 14, 2002 and February 20, 2003.

[40] See s.2(3) and s.2(6).

[41] See the evidence research by the Centre for Family Studies at the University of Newcastle, the key findings of which are available on the website of the Lord Chancellor's Department at www.open.gov.uk/lcd.

[42] For more detail see B. Kearney, *Children's Hearings and the Sheriff Court*, (2nd edn) Butterworths (2000); K. Norrie, *Children's Hearings in Scotland*, Greens, Edinburgh (1997).

[43] The basic age limit is age 16 but children over 16 in respect of whom a supervision order remains in force may be subject to the hearing system until age 18. For children charged with serious offences in criminal courts the disposal of a case after conviction can be remitted to the hearing.

[44] Though the Kilbrandon Report (1964) Cmnd 2306 para.3 suggests that they owe more than a fleeting indebtedness to the Scandinavian system of welfare bonds.

[45] Though expenses are paid by the local authority. Lord Penrose in *S v Miller* 2001 SLT 531 expressed a commonly held sentiment when he noted (at page 551) 'if there are deficiencies in the system, they are structural and do not reflect adversely on the dedication of the volunteers who carry out this work'.

[46] Termed Children's Panel Advisory Panels, Sch.1 Children (Scotland) Act,1995. The

panel has to include a male and female representative. The system was originally heavily local authority based although the introduction of the Scottish Children's Reporters Administration in 1994[47] gave a national focus to the scheme. However, it is still the local authority which sets up the Children's Panel Advisory Committee, pays their expenses, undertakes the investigation of cases on the request of the reporter,[48] pays the fees of safeguarders mentioned below, and determines the availability of certain dispositions. It is also predominantly (84%) the local authority's social workers' recommendations that determine the final decision.[49]

Its theoretical underpinning was the Kilbrandon Report[50] and its conclusion that whether children had offended or were in need of protection, they might be equally in need of what are termed special education and training (in the widest sense of education and training)[51] and the solution in practically every case involved working with the children's family.[52] Compulsory measures of supervision or training were necessary to meet those social or psychological needs which the children's family or school were not meeting.[53] Initially, the proceedings were expected to be primarily about children who had committed offences, with the protection cases being something of an afterthought. However, over time the percentage of offence referrals has declined as a percentage of the total caseload, whilst that of the non-offence cases has increased.[54] This has also affected the validity of the initial belief that an informal discussion[55] between the panel members, the parents and the child was the appropriate forum to resolve offence cases since the parents were expected to be part of the

---

panels are based on Local Authority areas, though smaller areas may combine together with the Approval of the Secretary of State.

[47] Local Government (Scotland) Act 1994 Part III.

[48] See below for a description of the reporter.

[49] See Scottish Office Social Work Findings No.25, *Deciding in Children's Interests* (1998).

[50] Report of the Committee on *Children and Young Persons*, Scotland Cmnd.2306 (1964). For the history of the Committee see D. J. Cowperthwaite, *The Emergence of the Scottish Children's Hearing System* (1988), Institute of Criminal Justice, University of Southampton. (Cowperthwaite was the Assistant Secretary of the Criminal Justice Division of the Scottish Home Department – later the Scottish Home and Health Department).

[51] Kilbrandon Report, para 13.

[52] Ibid., paras 252-254.

[53] See Kilbrandon Report, para. 15. It is perhaps not unexpected that Waterhouse and McGhee's study *Children in Focus*, summarised in *Children's Hearings in Scotland: compulsion and disadvantage* (2002) 24 J.S.W. & F.L. 279, found that the majority of children subject to compulsory measures were likely to come from backgrounds characterised by social disadvantage.

[54] By 1999/2000 the protection grounds constituted 65.3% of all referrals for girls and 36.7% for boys. The 1989 figure for both sexes was that protection grounds constituted only 24.8% of referral grounds. Scottish Children's Reporter Administration Statistical Bulletins 1997-2000.

[55] According to the empirical evidence (Scottish Office Social Work Research Findings No 25 *Deciding in the Children's Interests*) the involvement of the parents and children, beyond being present was limited. Their contributions were brief and they were nervous and only partly aware of their rights.

solution. However, in the case of protection grounds, particularly involving the child as a victim of a sexual offence, abuse or neglect,[56] the reality is both that the family may be the problem and that, as explained below, the family may wish to contest the allegations and take the case to court.

The decision about whether to refer a child to a Children's Hearing is to be taken by a person termed the reporter,[57] acting on referrals from the police, social workers, voluntary agencies or even members of the public. The scheme was implemented by the Social Work (Scotland) Act, 1968 but significantly changed by the Children (Scotland) Act 1995.

The Children's Hearings, however, were only to deal with investigations of cases and dispositions of cases where the essential facts about whether an offence had been committed[58] or whether a child was in need of protection were admitted. Since the hearings were not courts of law, disputes about facts were for adjudication by the sheriff court, and only when an adjudication had been made that an offence had been committed or that a child was in need of protection, would a case be referred to the Children's Hearing system.

The role of the Children's Hearings includes dealing with children charged with criminal offences up to age 16,[59] though in serious cases involving alleged child offenders below that age the Lord Advocate may issue instructions for the prosecution of the cases in the ordinary criminal courts.[60] Even in cases of serious crime other than

---

[56]   The Annual Report of the Scottish Children's Reporter Administration for 2001, published March 28, 2002 and summarised in *The Times* for March 29, 2002 revealed a 50% increase in abuse and neglect cases over the past 3 years which it attributed *inter alia* to parental alcohol and drug abuse as well as violence.

[57]   Such a person need not be legally qualified (s.40 Children (Scotland) Act 1995) and indeed many are drawn from teaching and social work or behavioural science backgrounds. However in the light of increasing legal and human rights issues some authors have argued that the position may need to be restricted to legally qualified persons (see A. Kelly, *Introduction to the Scottish Children's Panel,* Waterside Press, Winchester, (1996) p.72 or, Edwards suggests *op.cit.* infra. p.191 in the case of non-legally qualified reporters they could themselves be represented by a lawyer.

[58]   Certainly where serious offences were committed by children, the Lord Advocate retained the right to prosecute such children in the criminal courts.

[59]   In the Scottish Executive's *Youth Crime Review* published April 2002 (see electronic version at www.scotland.gov.uk/youth/crimereview) an appendix dealt with the desirability of developing a coherent bridging system between the Hearings and criminal justice systems. This would involve the development of pilot schemes by which the Procurator Fiscal referred increased numbers of cases involving criminal activity by 16- and 17-year-olds to the Children's Hearing System unless the youth involved created a risk to the public or his own safety. It was expected that this could address the abrupt transition between youths with a maturation problem (the temporary delinquent) from the supportive Children's Hearing system to the criminal justice system. The search for a more community based holistic solution to such youths was expected to require a multidisciplinary approach involving employment, education and training, housing and leisure facilities. It was hoped that the increased cost would be met by giving Local Authorities 'ring-fenced' Scottish Executive grants.

[60]   See Criminal Procedure (Scotland) Act 1995 s.42 and the special procedures relating

murder proved against under 16-year-olds in the ordinary criminal courts there is provision for involvement of the Children's Hearing system. Where the child is already on supervision the High Court *may*, and the sheriff court *must* seek the advice of the Principal Reporter about the treatment of the child. Even where the child is not already on supervision the court seized of the matter may remit the case to the Principal Reporter for either disposal or advice.[61]

The venue for adjudication of cases involving children is separate from the issue of the age of criminal responsibility which in Scotland is the very low age of 8.[62] On January 14, 2002[63] the Scottish Executive announced its decision to implement a recommendation of the Scottish Law Commission to raise the age of criminal responsibility to 12 as a way of ensuring that Scots law complies with the European Convention on Human Rights. Children under 12 who commit what would have been offences had they been old enough, would be dealt with in Children's Hearing proceedings under protection grounds. There have also been moves to raise (to 17) the age at which young people cease to be subject to the Children's Hearing system.[64]

---

to the arrest and detention of children under age 16 set out in ss.43-46. The current directions issued by the Lord Advocate are dated March 1996 (see Kearney, *Children's Hearings and the Sheriff Court* 2nd edn. (2000) Butterworths, Edinburgh, and include three categories of case: (i) proceedings prosecuted on indictment, such as murder or rape; (ii) offences committed by children 15 or over which on conviction oblige or permit a court to order disqualification from driving; (iii) certain offences committed by children between 16 and 18 covered by Children (Scotland) Act s.93(2)(b). The number of cases involving children heard in the High Court is probably only 0.5% (105 children in 1999) of the total caseload of children involved with the criminal justice system. For more detail see the Scottish Law Commission Report 185 on *The Age of Criminal Responsibility* H.M.S.O. Edinburgh Jan 2002 at p.29. Such cases do, however, pose particular problems about how adult criminal courts can be made more suitable for the small number of children brought before them. See the Damilola Taylor case in England (verdict April 26 2002) and the E.H.R.R. case of *T v. U.K.*; *V v. U.K.* 30 EHRR 121 which influenced the changes procedures in the Damilola Taylor case.

[61]   See Criminal Procedure (Scotland) Act 1995, s.49.

[62]   See Sutherland, *Child and Family Law* T & T Clark 1999 p.110, para 3.86 and her indication that this fact was not lost on the Monitoring Committee charged with monitoring the U.K.'s implementation of its responsibilities under the U.N. Convention on the Rights of the Child.

[63]   See *The Scotsman* for that date and critical comments from the Association of Scottish Police Superintendents. The Official Scottish Law Commission Report 185 on *The Age of Criminal Responsibility*, H.M.S.O. Edinburgh January 2002 provides more detail.

[64]   See *Making Scotland Safer*, Scottish Executive (2001) and *Youth Crime Review* Scottish Executive (2001) (www.scotland.gov.uk/pages/news 2002) and the proposals in the Criminal Justice (Scotland) Act 2003 to introduce this. On January 21, 2003 the Minister of Justice announced pilot measures for a two year period to enable a Youth Court to deal with repeat offenders by means of a fast track process with intensive disposals specifically designed for young offenders. The Youth Court proposals were primarily designed for 16 and 17 years olds with the flexibility to deal in some cases with 15 year olds. Similar proposals were announced on January 31, 2003 by the Minister of Education for pilot fast track focused disposal

The ostensible reason for this is to reduce the burden on District Courts by providing for those under 17 to be dealt with in a way better suited to dealing with young persons than the criminal courts. Critics[65] have emphasised that the Children's Hearing System has not been adequately funded by Local Authorities and Central Government and that since many of the more innovative solutions to juvenile problems have been available in parts of Scotland, but not others, the tying of the system to the Local Authority system without ring-fenced Central Government funding has led to a 'patchwork quilt effect'.[66] Recent increased funding by the Scottish Executive is aimed at alleviating this problem[67] but time will tell whether the efforts have been successful.

---

of cases involving repeat offenders brought before Children's Hearings. The proposals were coupled with an announcement (January 17, 2003) of an accreditation panel to promote community supervision programmes aimed at reducing youth re-offending.

[65] See *The Scotsman* February 18, 2002 for the assertion that this increase in work load will be the straw that breaks the camel's back and that the system is inadequately funded. Whilst recognising the funding problems Local Government and the Scottish Executive have sought to pin the blame on each other.

[66] Some innovative projects such as the Freagarrach Scheme in Central Region for separating out 'one off' young offenders from persistent offenders (5 or more episodes in offending in 12 months), predominantly male, with a history of substance abuse and from unhappy or disrupted family backgrounds are not available Scotland wide. The project involved intensive engagement with the offenders (three 1.5 -2.5 hour sessions a week) to engage the offenders in their offending and the reasons for it for a six week period. This was followed by an individual programme contract with specified targets for change and each party to the contract made commitments and specified the methods to be used to achieve change. Recreational activities were used as rewards for commitment to the programme which lasted for a period of 8-12 months. For more details see Freagarrach, *An Evaluation of a Project for Young Offenders* which is available on www.scotland.gov.uk/cru/kd01/green/freagarrach. Equally the innovative restorative justice scheme sponsored by SACRO and based predominantly on Australasian experience for a meeting between a victim and an offender at which the offender apologises to the victim and makes an offer to make good the damage SACRO, is again not offered on Scotland wide basis. (For more details see the paper 'SACRO'S Youth Justice Services'). Such schemes are said to reduce the quantity and seriousness of offending behaviour by forcing young people to confront the very real and serious human consequences of their actions. The referral criteria for the SACRO restorative justice program includes (i) the offender being between age 9-17 years; (ii) their residing in the area covered by the scheme; (iii) their having been charged with committing a criminal offence in which the Children's Hearing Reporter considers there is evidence meeting the criminal standard of proof; (iv) no more than 3 months has passed between the offence being committed and the date of referral to the Reporter; and (v) there must be an identifiable victim. Victim offender mediation with reparation raises the important issue about whether schemes sponsored or organised by agencies with a rehabilitation of the offender remit can adequately protect the interests of the victim and whether the children's hearing system is an appropriate mechanism for administering such schemes.

[67] See the Scottish Executive's Action Programme to Reduce Youth Crime 2002.

This informality of the Children's Hearing system of dealing with child offenders or victims should not mask the range of important decisions that could be made by the Children's Hearing system. Amongst the dispositions that are open to the hearing to recommend are the confinement of the child in secure accommodation. It was therefore inevitable that with the growth of human rights laws, various aspects of the system have recently come under scrutiny.

In 1991 Sanford Fox, one of the drafters of the United Nations Convention on the Rights of the Child, criticised the lack of availability of legal aid (as opposed to legal advice) for children and parents at hearings.[68] This resulted in the U.K. initially entering a long reservation about the Children's Hearing system when it ratified the U.N. Convention on the Rights of the Child, though this was later withdrawn.[69] Some protection for the child was afforded by the introduction in 1975[70] of a power by Children's Hearings and sheriffs, where they think it necessary, to appoint an independent person to safeguard the interests of the child by (i) assisting the child in expressing his or her views and (ii) presenting an independent analysis of what will serve the child's best interest. The tension between the two functions is obvious and is clearly different from that of legal representation for the child. The appointment of a safeguarder is not mandatory, and even when appointed the fee paid by local authorities is well below that of legal aid rates paid to solicitors.

With the advent of the operation of the Human Rights Act 1998, further aspects of the Children's Hearing system began to attract scrutiny. Norrie[71] supported Fox's argument that the right conferred by Art. 6(3)(2) of the European Convention of Human Rights for a person charged with an offence to defend himself or herself with legal assistance might be breached by the Children's Hearing system's refusal to provide legally aided representation for those involved in hearings. Norrie also argued that legal aid was required by European Court of Human Rights case-law in complex cases[72] as well as that relating to 'equality of arms' in adversarial proceedings. Two other criticisms were made by Rose.[73] First, the role of the reporter required scrutiny. It is the reporter who decides to refer the case to the hearing; in practice it is he (or she) who advises the panel about legal or other matters at the hearing;[74] and it is he (or she) who presents the case in the sheriff court if the grounds of referral are contested. Secondly, the children's hearing might not be independent as required by Art. 6 of the European Court of Human Rights. Although the members are independent in that once appointed they can only be removed by the First Minister with the consent of the Lord President,[75] the Children's Hearing only has the power to make a recommendation in relation to placement of a child in secure accommodation. Such a

---

68   (1991) Kilbrandon Child Care Lecture, Scottish Office, Edinburgh 1991.

69   Reservation F was withdrawn on April 17, 1997.

70   Children Act 1975 s.66.

71   K. Norrie, *Human Rights Challenges to the Children's Hearing System*, April 2000 J.L.S.S. 19.

72   See *Airey v Ireland* (1979) 2 E.H.R.R. 305.

73   J. Rose, *E.C.H.R. and the Children's Hearing System*, August 2000 Scolag 11.

74   See also the criticisms made by Kearney in (1985) 4 Civil Justice Quarterly 137 at 143-44.

75   See Tribunals and Inquiries Act 1992, s.7.

decision is, in effect, only made when the chief social work officer and the manager of the unit agree with this recommendation.[76] Moreover, when authorising non secure residential placements, as in a children's home, a hearing is, in practice, subject to the practical constraint that such an order can only be made where there is a children's home willing to take a child in.[77] The reality is that the Children's Hearing may be heavily dependent on the resources a local authority is prepared to make available for children's homes (or other dispositions) and even its philosophy towards closing children's homes in favour of other placements.[78] Even discounting the practicality point just made, given the dependence of the Children's Hearing on local authority consent before making secure accommodation orders, Norrie suggests, relying on *Benthem v Netherlands*,[79] that the restrictions on dispositions breaches Art.6.

Some, but not all, of these problems were resolved by the decision of the Inner House of the Court of Session in *S v Miller*.[80] S was a 17-year-old who had been involved in an assault in which a third party was injured and S's father was so seriously injured that he died some months later. S was arrested but after deliberation the procurator fiscal decided that the appropriate course was for the matter to be considered by the local Children's Hearing[81] at which the ground of referral to the hearing was that S had committed an offence under s.52(2)(i) of the Children (Scotland) Act 1995, the successor provisions to those originally found under the Social Work (Scotland) Act 1986. At this hearing,[82] S and his mother rejected the ground of referral but alleged, before the matter was sent for proof to the sheriff court for proof, that the Children's Hearing system did not comply with the European Convention on Human Rights.

A crucial issue in the light of the European Court of Human Rights decision in *Ozturk v Germany*[83] was whether the Children's Hearing relating to the assault

---

76   See Children (Scotland) Act 1995 s.70(9).

77   See Kearney op.cit. (2000) para.25.30.

78   It was the reluctance of the Fife Social Work Department to include certain types of accommodation and dispositions in its child care policy that led to the creation of *The Report of the Inquiry into Child Care* Policies in Fife (the Kearney Report) Edinburgh H.M.S.O. (1992). See the Prologue for the background.

79   (1985) 8 E.H.R.R. 1. Although *Benthem* was not a family law case (and in fact involved a statutory licensing scheme to supply petroleum gas for motor vehicles) the ECHR nevertheless held that a body which merely had a power of tendering advice which the Netherlands Crown was free to depart from was not a determination by a tribunal which complied with Art.6(1).

80   2001 SLT 531 analysed by Edwards, *S v Miller: The End of Children's Hearings System As We Know It?* 2002 SLT (News) 187.

81   Thus ending the possibility of any criminal charge; see Lord President Rodger's comments in *S v Miller* (ibid at p.540 F).

82   The hearing was in fact a second hearing- at the first hearing S had received advice from a solicitor who was not present at it. By the time of the second hearing S had again had legal advice and assistance but he had no solicitor present at the hearing-though his solicitor was in the same building.

83   (1984) 6 E.H.R.R. 409. The ECHR in *Ozturk* had emphasised that it was necessary to note for purposes of Art.6(1) not merely whether the proceedings were classified as non-criminal for the purpose of domestic law but consideration of the nature and

constituted criminal proceedings, in which case the right to legal aid would have been ensured by Art. 6(3)(c) of the European Convention of Human Rights. The Court unanimously held that the proceedings were merely ones in which S's civil rights and obligations were determined – though these still attracted the procedural protection of a right to 'a fair and public hearing by an independent and impartial tribunal' in Art. 6(1) of the Convention. Although the Court held that S had been originally charged with something which was clearly a criminal offence under Scots law, the nature of Children's Hearings, even when the offence ground was invoked, was civil *sui generis*.[84] This still left two other criteria from *Ozturk*,[85] namely, the nature of the offence and the nature and severity of any penalty attaching to the offence. Lord Rodger noted that where the offence ground was concerned, the standard of proof, the treatment of evidence and the applicability of the Rehabilitation of Offenders Act 1974 provisions all pointed to such proceedings being criminal proceedings. However, the fact that the proceedings were initiated by the Reporter rather than the procurator fiscal, that the dispositions were measures aimed at protecting the child's welfare rather than a imposing a criminal sentence, and the fact that appeals went through the civil route ending with the Inner House of the Court of Session rather than the High Court of Justiciary in its appellate form, suggested that these were not criminal proceedings or ones attaching criminal penalties,[86] even when, as Lord Penrose pointed out, secure accommodation conditions were imposed.[87] These he was prepared to classify as a protection for the child rather than as a punishment.

The mere fact that the hearings were not criminal ones still left the issue of whether the proceedings were a determination of the child's civil rights and obligations under Art. 6(3). The likelihood in a case like this was that S faced a real possibility of a secure accommodation order bringing about loss of liberty. Even a placement away from home with foster parents under a residential supervision requirement would affect the child's family rights. Compliance with Art. 6(1) required that such an order could only be made when made within a reasonable time by an independent and impartial tribunal established by law after a fair and public hearing. The independence of the tribunal did not seem to create much of a problem since panel members are appointed for 5 years and almost invariably reappointed.[88] A bigger problem is that, although after *McMichael v U.K.*[89] practice and the Children Hearings Rules 1996[90] were changed to allow parents and 'relevant persons' access to reports presented at the

---

severity of the penalty had also to be considered.

84   See *McGregor v D* 1977 SLT 182. Having regard to the difficulty in the classification of children's hearings on the offence ground perhaps civil OR *sui generis* might be more appropriate.

85   Ibid.

86   See Lord Rodger's comments at p.538.

87   At p.556.

88   See Lord Rodger at p.556 J, noting that no member has been refused reappointment save where they have declined to take part in necessary training. The mere fact that the panel members were unpaid does not seem to have been a concern, whereas the fact that they were chosen because of their special training (both before and during their appointment) in legal and child care seems to have carried more weight.

89   (1995) E.H.R.R. 205.

90   S.I. 2361 (S.251).

hearing rather than a mere verbal summary from the chairperson of the hearing,[91] such rights were still not available to the child himself, even when a presumptively mature child of 12. In order to meet the criticisms of Norrie (and others),[92] the Principal Reporter indicated in draft guidance notes that the child should receive these save where their release might prejudice crime prevention or detection or cause serious harm to the child.[93]

The lack of legal aid for the hearings, criticised for many years by Sanford Fox[94] and others, gave rise to bigger problems in the light of the European Court of Human Rights case in *Airey v Ireland*,[95] which indicated that at least in serious cases a state might be obliged, in the interest of 'equality of arms' to provide free legal aid in serious cases. Applying the European Court of Human Rights, the Inner House concluded that there was a breach especially given that many of the children involved with the hearing system might be young, given the present Scottish age of criminal responsibility, and the fact that young children with medical or psychological problems would be at a disadvantage at the hearing without legal representation. *Airey* had never required legal aid across the board in civil cases and thus the crucial issue is when are the issues serious enough to require the grant of legal aid. Lord Penrose suggested this might be likely where (i) the making of a secure accommodation order was likely; (ii) cases involving very young children or children with limited intelligence or social skills; or (ii) cases involving difficult legal issues such as self defence, provocation.[96] Beyond that there might be cases not covered by the three listed cases where the complexity of the case required in *Airey* terms the appointment of a lawyer. Edwards suggests that in some cases, e.g. where a relevant person of limited intelligence is alleged to have perpetrated abuse on the child, then the perpetrator may require this. One instance might be where a sibling of the victim is the alleged perpetrator.[97] The Scottish Executive moved to remedy the problem by

---

91   See Rule 5(3) of the Children's Hearing Rules 1996, in conjunction with s.93(2)(b) of the Children (Scotland) Act 1995, though note that the father of a child born out of wedlock is not a relevant person unless he had acquired parental responsibilities and rights under a court order made under s.11 of the Act or has acquired PRR under a written parental rights agreement in prescribed form and registered in the Books of Council and Session (the Scottish public register for important private legal agreements).

92   2000 J.L.S.S. 21.

93   Ibid., at p.542 E. Had the concession not been made Lord Penrose concluded that a declaration of incompatibility might have been called for (p.560 F).

94   See *ante*.

95   (1979) 2 E.H.R.R.305.

96   Ibid., at p.562 A-D. Since all these circumstances were present on the facts of the instance case they probably should be regarded as exhaustive. Indeed Lord Penrose adverted to the possibility under the existing law of reports being produced after the grounds of referral has been admitted or established alleging criminal behaviour of a child which had been neither accepted by the child not established before the sheriff and which might require future consideration. See Children's Hearings (Legal Representation)(Scotland) Rules 2002 (SSI 2002/63).

97   See the NCH Report *Children Sexually Abusing Other Children* (1992).

passing the Children's Hearings (Legal Representation)(Scotland) Rules 2002[98] which permits the award of legal aid.[99] A cheaper alternative might be for an increase in the appointment of safeguarders, though given the tension between the safeguarder's function to relay the child's wishes to the court and the function of providing an independent assessment of what the child's interest might require (which might be quite different), care would need to be taken before deciding that a safeguarder might be an adequate substitute for legally aided legal representation.[100]

Other areas of Human Rights challenge to the Children's Hearing system still exist. Whilst placement of a child away from home is not lightly to be undertaken, it is permitted under the provisions of s.70 of the Children (Scotland) Act 1995 relating to supervision with a residential condition. As Sheriff Kearney points out, such a decision will be affected by the resources available, and the inclusion of a requirement that a child will reside in a named establishment should be reserved to cases where the establishment concerned is willing and has a vacancy for the child.[101] Where a local authority refuses to make such residential accommodation available or in sufficient numbers, considerable problems can occur and the panel members may feel impotent.[102] Even more important than the practical restrictions on the hearing are the legal ones relating to the authorization of secure accommodation for a child by the Children's Hearing under s.70(9) of the Children (Scotland) Act 1995. Such a recommendation is not an order at all but merely authorises the manager of the unit with the agreement of the Chief Social Work Officer to hold the child.[103] Norrie[104] suggests that implicit in the concept of an independent tribunal is the ability to make decisions and if the Hearing cannot make what it thinks is an order necessary to protect the child from a risk of physical, mental or moral risk, it is not independent as required under s.6. The reality is that the Children's Hearing system, both as it affects the panel and children and families they deal with, provides a veneer of legality to a

---

[98]   SSI 2002/63 effective February 22, 2002.
[99]   The representative must be a solicitor on the panel of safeguarders or curators *ad litem* or reporting officers.
[100]   Sutherland is now of this view having expressed a different opinion earlier. See Sutherland in Sutherland and Cleland (ed), *Children's Rights in Scotland* (2nd ed) (2001) W.Green, Edinburgh, p. 295 and especially f.n. 10.
[101]   See Kearney, *Children's Hearings and the Sheriff Court* (2nd edn.) Butterworths, Edinburgh, (2000) pp.300 et seq.
[102]   See *The Report of the Inquiry into Child Care Policies in Fife (Kearney Report)* H.M.S.O Edinburgh (1992) for an example of this problem. The children's panel's fears that children were kept at risk by being kept out of care led to Sheriff Kearney finding that there were serious causes for concern about the way in which the child care policies in Fife were being implemented and the Director of Social Work's policies were described as over simplified, dogmatic and rigid. The Director of Social Work moved on and became Director of Social Care and Health in Brighton only to resign after controversies over the death of a child in which proper procedures had allegedly not been followed by social workers in relation to supervising the child's adoptive parents (see *Dundee Courier* April 12 2002).
[103]   Secure Accommodation (Scotland) Regs. 1996 SI 1996/3255 r.6.
[104]   2000 J.L.S.S. 19 at p.20 suggests, relying in part on *Bentham v Netherlands* (1985) 8 E.H.R.R. 1, the fact that it can make binding decisions.

system heavily dependent on the decisions of the Social Work Department and the resourcing available to it, and so there is clearly an element of truth in this argument but given the attachment of the judiciary to the system one suspects it may not win the day.

A more likely source of successful challenge lies in the multiple role of the reporter. The consistent reporter not merely provides the administration for the system and acts as gate keeper to it, but also (as a matter of practice rather than law) advises the hearing on legal matters,[105] conducts the case at the sheriff court if the grounds of referral are contested and, under the newly passed Children's Hearings (Legal Representation) Rules 2002,[106] decides whether to arrange a business meeting to appoint a legal representative for the child and to release any documents to such an appointee.

Norrie[107] suggests that at the Sheriff Court the reporter is entirely disinterested in the outcome and is completely independent of the Social Work Department and that this is not open to attack.[108] However, he continues 'more vulnerable is the reporter's role at grounds of referral hearings' and he suggests that the way forward would be for the grounds of referral to be accepted before the sheriff. An alternative might be for the Clerk to the District Court (Magistrates Court) to attend Children's Hearings to answer any legal questions which the hearing may have.

There is a final problem with the Children's Hearing system, though not in Human Rights Act terms, namely, that there is a need for imaginative dispositions to be available on a Scotland wide basis. Recently the Principal Reporter talked of a need for something more than periodic meetings of the child and his or her social worker. Instead he urged the introduction, monitoring and evaluation of alternative approaches such as challenging offending behaviour, victim offender mediation, and alcohol and drug abuse programmes.[109] However, imaginative dispositions like requiring the child to attend programs like Freagarrach or victim offender mediation[110] are available only in some regions of Scotland. In March 2002 there was an announcement that a voluntary scheme by which offenders might have to meet their victims to apologise to them and make an act of restitution to them to ameliorate the loss they had caused might be introduced gradually over the whole of Scotland. Such a scheme borrowed from Australia and New Zealand is alleged to force offenders to confront their behaviour and its effect on the victim in a way that is not a 'soft option' for the offender.[111]

---

[105] In the *Laws of Scotland*, Stair Memorial Encyclopedia Volume 3, Butterworths (1994) para.1317 it is argued that the Reporter should only offer advice in response to request from the panel members.

[106] *supra.*

[107] *op. cit.*

[108] Though because the decision to end the Hearing is for panel members rather than the Reporter, Professor Black has argued (address to the Children's Panel National School in November 1999) that the Reporter might be alleged to have an interest in the outcome of the proceedings.

[109] See Alan Miller, the Principal Reporter's address, to the Youth Crime in Scotland on October 9, 2001.

[110] See f.n. 66 *ante.*

[111] See SACRO's *Youth Justice Services* mentioned in f.n. 66 *ante.*

Chapter 5

'Please, Sir, I want some more': New Developments in the South African Saga of Child Maintenance and Children's Rights

Brigitte Clark

Introduction

During the past three years,[1] the position of poverty-stricken children in South Africa has not improved. In this country, a growing perception has developed that spending on social welfare services (as opposed to direct transfer payments in the form of grants and pensions) has diminished in the period since 1996.[2] The lack of resources for both the prevention of abuse and neglect and for the protection of children is a central issue of concern in South Africa. There are, however, indications that the Constitutional Court and law reformers may well force the Government to take more dramatic steps than it has hitherto done. The implications of the South African ratification of the United Nations Convention on the Rights of the Child (CRC),[3] the constitutionalisation of children's rights,[4] recent Constitutional and Supreme Court of Appeal cases and the new South African Children's Bill and Discussion Paper preceding it indicate that the state can no longer assume that social problems can be located solely within the individual or the family.

It is estimated that by 2005 there will be more than 1 million children under 16 years of age who have lost their parents due to HIV/AIDS,[5] and that by 2010 there

---

[1] See Brigitte Clark, *Child Maintenance and the South African State* (2000) 8 International Journal on Children's Rights 307.

[2] See South African Law Commission Discussion paper 13 *Review of the Child Care Act 74 of 1983* Project 110 (2002) Chapter 25, p.1260.

[3] June 1995.

[4] Section 28 of the Constitution of the Republic of South Africa 108 of 1996.

[5] This is the term commonly used for the human immunodeficiency virus (HIV) leading to the acquired deficiency syndrome (AIDS).

will be more than 2 million children under the age of 16 who have been orphaned by the disease.[6] South Africa has a population of about 42 million. Approximately one-third of all South African households, about 18 million people, are living below the poverty line.[7] Thirty-five per cent of South African households are headed by women and, of those households, 65 per cent live below the poverty datum line.[8] There are 17 million children under the age of 18 in South Africa, which constitutes almost half of the population. Two thirds of all children live in fairly remote rural areas, and half of all children do not even possess birth certificates.[9]

The effect of the constitutionalisation of children's rights and the United Nations Convention on the Rights of the Child

The South African Constitution provides that everyone has the right to have access to social security, including, if they are unable to support themselves and their dependants, appropriate social assistance.[10] The State is obliged to take reasonable legislative and other measures, within its available resources, to achieve progressive realisation of this right.[11] Section 28(1)(c) of the Constitution refers directly to the child's rights to basic social services, and it has been alleged that 'there is a close link between social security and social services rights'.[12] The CRC provides an indication as to what social services should be provided for children by States Parties which have ratified that Convention.[13] These include protecting children from physical or mental violence, injury or abuse, neglect or negligent treatment, and protecting children against economic exploitation.[14]

---

[6]   See IDASA Budget Brief *An Evaluation of the Department of Social Development's Response to the HIV/AIDS Crisis* (2001) p.10.

[7]   Ministry of Welfare and Population Development White Paper for Social Welfare (1997).

[8]   See address by Deputy Minister of Justice, Cheryl Gilwald at Du Toit Conference on *Changing Family Patterns* (unpublished paper) March 25, 2002.

[9]   Shirin Motala *Children in South Africa: A contextual analysis*, An unpublished paper presented at the National Workshop on Social Security for Children in South Africa, March 7 and 8, 2001.

[10]   Section 27(1)(c) of the Constitution of the Republic of South Africa Act 108 of 1996.

[11]   Section 27(2).

[12]   S. Liebenberg and K. Pillay *Socio-economic Rights in South Africa* (Community Law Centre) University of the Western Cape (2000) at p.324. See too S. Liebenberg *The Protection of Economic and Social Rights in Domestic Legal Systems* in A. Eide et al., *Economic Social and Cultural Rights*, Kluwer, The Netherlands (2001).

[13]   In articles 26 and 27.

[14]   In its concluding observations on the First Country Report submitted by the South African Government to the Committee on the Rights of the Child, the Committee urged the South African government to extend the reach of the provision of social

The South African constitution incorporates a number of socio-economic rights, for example s.28(1)(c) places an obligation on the State to provide children with access to shelter, basic nutrition, basic health care and social services. In the landmark decision of *The Government of the Republic of South Africa v. Grootboom and Others*,[15] the Constitutional Court of South Africa acknowledged the need for the South African government to develop a policy to ensure that every effort is made to comply with these constitutionally incorporated socio-economic rights. The court *a quo* in this case had interpreted s.28(1)(c) of the South African Constitution as bestowing upon evicted children of squatters the right to shelter at the state's expense. However, on appeal, the Constitutional Court was at pains to stress that the carefully constructed constitutional scheme for the progressive realisation of socio-economic rights would make little sense if it could be trumped in every case by the rights of children to get shelter from the state on demand. The Constitutional Court was careful to emphasise that the children's rights clause did *not* create independent rights. In the view of the court, all the children's rights clause did was to ensure that children were properly cared for by their families and that they received appropriate alternative care in the absence of family or parental care: the state did not have the primary obligation to provide shelter for children if the children were being cared for by their families.

The *Grootboom* case illustrates the relationship between every person's right to housing contained in s.26 of the South African constitution and children's right to shelter, as provided for in s.28(1)(c). The court held that there was an obvious overlap between the rights. Section 28(1)(c) and s.26 could not be regarded as establishing separate and distinct entitlements. The court held that s.28(1)(c) did not normally create a 'direct and enforceable' claim upon the State by children.[16] Section 28(1)(b) of the South African Constitution gives every child the right to 'family care or parental care or to appropriate alternative care when removed from the family environment'. This wording suggests that children living in child-headed households have a right to be provided with substitute parental or family care, or alternative care (such as institutional care). The court in *Grootboom* held that the rights enumerated in s.28(1)(c) should be interpreted in the context of the primary duty of parents towards their children as provided for in s.28(1)(b). Thus, the rights to 'basic nutrition, shelter, basic health care services and social services' encapsulate 'the scope of care that children should receive in our society',[17] while s.28(1)(b) ensures that children receive proper parental or familial care. However, although the court stressed that the primary responsibility for supporting children

---

security in the form of the Child Support Grant to children, and further to extend its availability to children aged above 7 years.

15   2001 (1) SA 46 (CC).
16   Para.74.
17   J. Sloth Nielsen, *Ratification of the Convention on the Rights of the Child: Implications for South Africa* (1985) South African Journal on Human Rights 331; J. Sloth Nielsen, *The Child's Right to Social Security and Primary Prevention of Child Abuse: Some Conclusions in the aftermath of Grootboom* 2001 (17) South African Journal on Human Rights 210.

rested on parents and families, it also emphasised that, where children are abandoned or lack a family environment, the State does bear the primary responsibility for providing for them. If one were to widen the context, this would imply that urgent measures need to be taken to provide state support and social services to children orphaned by HIV/AIDS.

The current maintenance and social security provisions for children

The South African maintenance system rests, on the one hand, on the judicial maintenance system which is based on the legal duty to support one's dependants, determined judicially where there is dispute.[18] On the other hand, there is the State maintenance system, which is meant to act as a safeguard by providing support where the procedures of the judicial maintenance system fail to do so. As far as the state maintenance system is concerned, there are three main types of child grant: child support grants (CSGs), foster care grants (FCGs) and care-dependency grants (CDGs).

The CSG was implemented in 1996 and is payable to primary care-givers of children who are under seven years.[19] A primary care-giver is defined as a person (whether related to the child or not), who takes primary responsibility for meeting the daily care needs of the child, but excludes a person who is paid (or an institution which received an award) to care for the child and also excludes a person who does not have the (express or implied) consent of the parent, guardian or custodian of the child. Presently, the 'take-up rate' for the CSG has increased from 30,000 children who benefited in 1998 to 1.2 million children by April 2001.[20] The Department of Social Development expects the take-up rate to exceed the projected target of reaching 3 million children aged below 7 years.[21] This indicates how few children are actually being assisted by the grant.[22] In August 2001, widespread reports of severe child malnutrition in the Eastern Cape were reported after a study conducted by the School of Public Health at the University of the Western Cape. Even where the Grant is being received, it is limited to children aged less than 7 years, and the amount payable is inadequate to address even children's basic needs.[23] There is no available financial relief for parents or children living in poverty where the children are aged over 7 years.

---

18 A recent ruling of the Constitutional Court expressed the concern of this court for the difficulties experienced by women and children in enforcing their rights under this system (see *Ballantyne v Ballantyne* unreported C.C.T.18/02 20 December 2002).

19 Welfare Amendment Act 106 of 1997.

20 Department of Social Development inputs to yearbook 2001/2002 at www.welfare.gov.za.

21 Ibid.

22 D. Budlender *Social Security and Grants* research paper commissioned by the South African Law Commission (1999).

23 The amount payable is to date R120 per month (approximately £10 per month).

A person is eligible for a Foster Care Grant (FCG) if he or she is a foster parent and qualifies in terms of the Act. The FCG has become the preferable child support grant for a number of reasons, including the increased amount,[24] and the fact that it is paid until the child is eighteen years old, while the CSG ends with the child's seventh birthday. In contrast to the CSG and other grants available in South Africa, the FCG is not means tested. Although some magistrates are reported to be reluctant to award this grant where children are placed with relatives, such as grandmothers,[25] there is no legal impediment to the payment of the FCG to relatives.[26]

A care-dependency grant (CDG) is available to a parent of a child under the age of eighteen who receives permanent home care due to severe disability. This, like the FCG, is payable until the child reaches the age of 18 years. After attaining the age of 18 years, a child beneficiary may apply for a disability grant. Like the FCG, there have been problems in regard to the payment of this grant due to the lack of clear criteria for the awarding of the grant, and the lack of a coherent definition of 'care dependency' with a consequent lack of uniformity in assessments of care dependent children.

Poverty and the effect of the HIV/AIDS epidemic on South Africa's children

The current situation of South African children living in extreme poverty indicates that 72% of children or 4.6 million aged 0-6, and 12.3 million aged 0-18 live in poverty.[27] On the absolute definition of child poverty that categorises a child as poor if he or she has income per month below the level estimated necessary to ensure a secure existence, just over half of the South African population earn less than $2 per day, and about 12 million people are very poor, existing on under $1 per day. This situation has been exacerbated by the impact of HIV/AIDS and there are reports of child-headed households with no access to food.[28] Unless such children are aged under 7, and living with a primary care-giver who can apply for a

---

24   G. O. Hollamby, *Submission to the Committee of Inquiry into a Comprehensive Social Security System*, unpublished paper delivered on 17 October 2000.

25   South Africa National Council for Child and Family Welfare, *Supplementary Report to the Committee of Inquiry into a Comprehensive Social Security System*, 29 November 2000.

26   Section 15(1)(b) of the Child Care Act 74 of 1983 permits the placement of a child 'into the custody of a suitable foster parent designated by the court under the supervision of a social worker' which indicates that there is no legislative distinction between placements with relatives as opposed to non-relatives.

27   See IDASA Budget Brief No.61 (2001) *Budget 2001 does little for child poverty*; Opening address by the Minister of Social Development at the National Conference on Children in Need of Special Protection, University of the Western Cape, Belville October 2001 (http/welfare.gov.za/ accessed November 12, 2001).

28   See for example *Mail and Guardian* October 26 – November 1, 2001 for a report on the National Children's Forum on HIV/Aids held in Cape Town on August 27 and 28, 2001.

CSG, or placed in formal foster care in order for the FCG to be payable, there is no monetary support available. Furthermore, children, who themselves are HIV/AIDS positive, are not regarded as competent to qualify for the CDG. Finally, the absence of effective measures to prevent maternal to child transmission of the virus has meant that 30-35 per cent of babies born to HIV infected women are themselves infected.[29]

There is an anti-retroviral drug called Nevirapine which is fast-acting and potent and can prevent transmission of HIV from mother-to-child interpartum. Its use is approved by the World Health Organisation and has been approved and registered in South Africa since 1998. Nevirapine had been demonstrated to halve the risk that pregnant women will transmit the virus to their children. Moreover, the cost of providing Nevirapine is less than the cost of treating HIV positive children, particularly since the offer by the manufacturer of a free five-years supply of Nevirapine. The drug has also been registered by the Medicine Control Council, which is of the view that the drug is safe and effective. Furthermore, one of the provinces in South Africa, the Western Cape, had been providing it on a much more widespread basis and reached 50 per cent of that province.

In January 2001, the South African Government at last agreed (tentatively) to the free treatment of HIV pregnant women and the provision of free anti-retroviral drugs for these women, but only as a pilot project in eighteen training pilot centres which would only reach 10 per cent of the population.

The gains made by this were offset by the announcement by the South African Department of Health that it would appeal against a court ruling brought by the Treatment Action Campaign ordering the government to provide the anti-retroviral drug Nevirapine to all HIV positive pregnant women giving birth at state institutions. Anti AIDS campaigners, such as the members of the Treatment Action Campaign, accused the government of deliberately hampering efforts to combat AIDS in South Africa, a country which has one of the highest number of persons infected in the world. In some areas of the Eastern Cape, medical staff became so desperate to administer this drug to pregnant women that one doctor has considered supplying it himself.[30]

In December 2001, a High Court of South Africa (per Botha J.), in response to an application brought against the Minister of Health by the Treatment Action Campaign, had ordered that the government had a duty to provide Nevirapine to pregnant women who were HIV-positive, giving birth in state institutions, where it was medically indicated and where there was capacity to do so.[31] This court also

---

[29]   I. Nicholl, A. Timaeus, R. M. Kigadye, G. Walveren and J. Killewo, *The Impact of HIV Infection on Mortality in Children under Five Years of Age in Sub-Saharan Africa: A Demographic and Epidemidogic Analysis*, AIDS (1994).

[30]   See Lynne Altenroxel, *State Aids Appeal puts more babies at risk*, *The Star* March 27, 2002. Dr. Conradie is the medical superintendent of Dordrecht Hospital in the Eastern Cape where at least every month one terminally ill baby is admitted. Had those mothers been given Nevirapine the death rate amongst the children could be halved. With every day that passes seventy-five babies who could have been saved by being given the drug will be born HIV positive.

[31]   See TPD case 21182/2001, unreported, per Botha J.

ruled against the present system of providing the medication only at certain pilot sites and ordered that the government present an outline of how it planned to extend provision of the medication to its birthing institutions countrywide. The state did not implement the order despite the convincing evidence that a comprehensive 'Mother to Child Transmission Programme' would result in a saving of resources in the public sector when compared to the costs associated with the illnesses and death of HIV positive children. The arguments presented by the TAC also indicated that, by failing to provide Nevirapine, the government was acting *ultra vires* its own policy[32] that entitles pregnant women and children under the age of 6 years to free health services.[33] By only making Nevirapine available selectively, the TAC argued that the Government was guilty of discrimination against the poor.[34] Furthermore, by placing effective drugs beyond the reach of most people in the country, the government was threatening the fundamental rights of South Africans to access to health care (s.27), basic health care services for children (s.28(1)(c), life (s.11), human dignity (s.10), equality (s.9) and psychological integrity, including the right to make decisions regarding reproduction (s.12(2)(a)). Finally, the applicants pointed to a breach of the State's positive obligation to promote access to health care in terms of s.27(2) of the Constitution.[35]

The TAC thus argued that the refusal of the South African government to set out a reasonable implementation plan for a Mother to Child transmission programme constituted a violation of the rights of access to health care, equality, life, dignity, reproductive choice and the rights of children as embodied in Chapter 2 of the Constitution of South Africa. Both the government and the court in the high court decision focussed on the right to health care (s.27 of the Constitution). The TAC relied on the *Grootboom* case[36] as imposing a positive duty on the part of the state to 'create the conditions for access to healthcare service for people at all economic levels of society'. In the High Court judgment, the court had held that *Grootboom's* case had been most instructive and followed the principles laid down in the case. The court held that the prohibition by the government on the use of Nevirapine outside the pilot sites in the public health section was not reasonable and constituted an unjustifiable barrier to the progressive realisation of the right to health care. The court, in examining the programme of the state found that there was no comprehensive and co-ordinated government plan for an extension of the mother to child transmission prevention programme. The court concluded that a countrywide mother to child transmission prevention programme was an 'ineluctable obligation of the state'. This ruling heightened the tension between the government and the judiciary.

---

32   See GN 657 of 1994.
33   See *Minister of Health and others v. Treatment Action Campaign and others* 2002 (5) S.A. 721 (CC); 2002 (10) B.C.L.R. 1033 (CC).
34   Ibid., para.1.11.3.
35   2001 (1) SA 46 (CC).
36   2001 (1) SA 46 (CC).

In response, the Government argued that only certain categories of patients are absolved from payment for health services and based their legal argument on the incapacity of the court to determine whether the government had a constitutional obligation to make Nevirapine available in the public sector in that the issue was only of health policy, not constitutional right and therefore not one for the courts to determine.[37] Any judicial review of its policy-making function, stated the Government, would result in a violation of the principle of separation of powers. The government's arguments thus implicitly questioned the justiciability of the socio-economic rights.

The South African Government then lodged an appeal with the Constitutional Court against this High Court decision.[38] This appeal was against the judge's decision that that section of the original judgment be implemented. In this first case, the Constitutional Court heard argument on the question of whether the state might appeal against the ruling that it execute Judge Botha's ruling and on April 4, the Constitutional Court dismissed the appeal, deciding that the state should comply.

The decision of the Constitutional Court[39] on the major issues of the Government's obligation to provide access to rights to housing, health care, food, water and social security is of great significance in the increasing socio-political conflict over the government's handling of South Africa's HIV/AIDS pandemic. The court's order represents a remarkable direct enforcement of the right to health care enshrined in s.27(1)(a) of the Constitution.[40] The court had to apply the test of reasonableness to determine whether the government's programme was consistent with its obligation in terms of s.27. The court identified two sets of criteria that could be used in assessing the rationality of the government's standpoint. In this regard, the court held that firstly, legislative action is insufficient and must be accompanied by appropriate, well-directed policies and programmes implemented by the Executive and secondly, *Grootboom's* case requires that accessibility should be progressively realised through the provision of facilities. It is only the pace of progressive realisation that is dictated by available resources.

The court thus came to the conclusion that the government's failure to develop a comprehensive and co-ordinated plan for an extension of the Mother to Child Transmission prevention plan cannot be justified either as one of several legitimate policy choices or by the claim that resources are insufficient. The cost of Nevirapine is now negligible; there is capacity within the public health care sector to extend the programme, as evidenced by the efforts of one province in particular

---

[37] In relying on this argument, the Government made reference to an earlier decision of *Soobramoney v. Minister of Health, KwaZulu-Natal* 1998 (1) SA 765 (CC), which in fact, dealt with a different right, the right not to be refused emergency medical treatment in terms of s.27(3), which the Constitutional Court held was subject to the realities of medical rationing and subject to limitations.

[38] *Minister of Health v Treatment Action Campaign* 2002 (5) SA 703 (CC).

[39] *Minister of Health v Treatment Action Campaign* 2002 (5) SA 721 (CC).

[40] Act 108 of 1996. See Heinz Klug, *Access to Heath Care: Judging Implementation in the Context of AIDS: Treatment Action Campaign v Minister of Health TPD 21182/2001 (unreported)* (2002) 18 South African Journal on Human Rights 114.

in managing to reach 50 per cent of the population of that province. The court's decision thus closely followed that laid down in the *Grootboom* case avoiding the critical question of just how far the government has to go to achieve the progressive realisation of a socio-economic right.[41]

New proposals: a new South African Children's Act[42]

The traditional nuclear family providing support for biological children is not a viable construct, in that increasingly fewer South African families live in this way. The South African State, via the Departments of Welfare and Justice and the courts, will have to assume increased responsibility for the maintenance of children, if it is to avoid substantial harm to its children. The South African Law Commission, in its recent Children's Bill, has made a number of proposals for preventative measures against malnutrition and in support of children in difficult circumstances or those living in child-supported households.

The South African Law Commission in its Discussion Document[43] took the view that, where the carer of the child is related to the child, a new category of care, namely 'care with relatives' should be introduced.[44] The Commission also recommended the establishment of grants aimed at subsidising adoptions to enable long-term foster care to be converted into the more secure and permanent option of adoption. If a grant was available to enable adoptions to be subsidised, this might encourage the development of community placements for at least some children who have been orphaned by HIV/AIDS. The South African Law Commission believed that the introduction of adoption grants would derive support from the ratio of the *Grootboom's* case since the Constitutional Court *in casu* stated that it regarded the State as bearing the primary responsibility (as regards the duty of support) where children lack a family environment, such as where they are orphaned, abandoned, or removed from their families. Where adoptive parents were unable to bear the additional costs attendant upon raising a child, it is possibly arguable that the State is obliged to assist them in terms of its primary obligation to support such children.

The South African Law Commission had also recommended the extension of the CSG to become a more universal social security system,[45] targeting all poor children aged under 18 years and not limited to children under the age of seven and stated that the current amount of the CSG is inadequate to enable care-givers to

---

41   See Heinz Klug, loc cit at p.123.

42   See Children's Bill (2002) which has as its objects the promotion of the protection, development and well-being of children.

43   See S.A.L.C. Discussion Paper 13 (Project 110).

44   G.O. Hollamby, *Placement of children in foster care with relatives*, unpublished submission to the Portfolio Committee on Social Development, November 22, 2001.

45   In line with the Committee on the Rights of the Child response to the South Africa country report which urged the Government of South Africa to consider extending the ambit of the child support grant.

provide for children's primary needs and proposes that the legislation require government to review the amount payable for the CSG on an annual basis, and to adjust it in line with the inflation rate.

Conclusion: A class action on behalf of children deprived of support and family care

The grants system and the recommendations concerning the broadening of access of children to state-provided social security will obviously have large-scale fiscal implications for the State. New approaches towards child maintenance are urgently required in South Africa, including the identification of a minimum core of the government's obligations in relation to this right. Every effort must be made to prevent administrative lack of fairness, delays and corruption in the delivery of child support to children. Such corruption is unfortunately very prevalent in the administrative departments of certain provinces of South Africa. [46]

In the Supreme Court of Appeal case of *The Permanent Secretary, Department of Welfare, Eastern Cape Government v Ngxuza*,[47] four individual applicants, assisted by the Legal Resources Centre (a non-governmental organisation of lawyers working to advance human rights) brought proceedings against the Eastern Cape government to reinstate the disability grants which they had been receiving and which the province had without notice to them terminated. The litigants were drawn from the poorest of South African society. Their claims were small: each claim would hardly secure them an hour of consultation with a lawyer and they were all victims of official excess, bureaucratic misdirection and unlawful administrative methods. The papers filed recount a 'pitiable saga of correspondence, meetings, calls, appeals and pleas by public interest organisations and even by branches of the African National Congress itself' (the governing party in the Eastern Cape).[48] Indeed, the court had hard and angry words to say about the behaviour of the Eastern Cape Government, describing them as 'contradictory, cynical, expedient and obstructionist'.

The court acknowledged that the poverty of many would-be litigants and the technicalities of legal procedure had led to the creation in the South African Constitution of the express entitlement that anyone asserting a right in the Bill of Rights could litigate as a member of or in terms of the interest of a group or class

---

[46]   See too *Mahambela v. MEC for Welfare, Eastern Cape, and Another* 2002 (1) SA 342 (SE) *and Mbanga v. MEC for Welfare, Eastern Cape, and Another* 2002 (1) SA 359 (SE) in which the court held that incidents of administrative inefficiency on the part of the Department of Welfare in this province were not isolated, but were 'the tip of the iceberg' in that in the recent months, numerous applications of the nature of these two cases had been brought against the Department of Welfare in the Eastern Cape.

[47]   2001 (4) SA 1184 (SCA).

[48]   See *Mahambela v. MEC for Welfare, Eastern Cape, and Another* 2002 (1) SA 342 (SE) *and Mbanga v. MEC for Welfare, Eastern Cape, and Another* 2002 (1) SA 359 (SE).

or person.[49] The Supreme Court of Appeal went on to adopt a generous interpretation to this section of the Constitution in order to give disadvantaged and poor people a chance to approach the courts on public issues to ensure the public administration adheres to the fundamental principle of legality in the exercise of public power. Thus, the case establishes an important precedent in such cases and might well lead to the institution of some type of class action on behalf of children deprived of any form of maintenance. This could have a very far-reaching impact on the development of human rights litigation in South Africa and opens the way for further action in South Africa on behalf of hitherto 'invisible litigants' such as children who are suffering from malnutrition as a result of bureaucratic inability to deliver the required (albeit inadequate) Child Support Grant.

The beginning of a period of children's rights public interest litigation may follow, especially in areas such as health, access to nutrition, and enforcement of the government's welfare responsibilities. As the *Treatment Action Campaign* case indicates, the South African government must not only have a plan to implement the progressive realisation of socio-economic rights, particularly where children are affected, but also that plan must examine how to progressively and *reasonably* assist the plight of the poverty-stricken so as to ensure that the South African constitution is based on real and not merely paper rights.

---

[49]   See s.38 of the Constitution of the Republic of South Africa Act 108 of 1996.

Chapter 6

The Care Standards Tribunal of England and Wales: A Contribution to Human Rights

His Honour Judge David Pearl

General background

This chapter describes the machinery that has now been put in place in England and Wales to hear appeals from those individuals who have been prohibited from working with children.[1] Initial decisions are taken as regards teachers by the Secretary of State for Education and Skills, and as regards social workers, by the Secretary of State for Health. Until recently such decisions were only susceptible of judicial review in the sense that the procedures could be investigated by the High Court. The merits of the decision however were not capable of any judicial investigation, except perhaps in the more exceptional case where it could be argued that the relevant Government department had reached a decision that no reasonable person would have reached.

Such an approach was understandable. Child protection policies inevitably were at the forefront of a strategy designed to ensure that our children are safeguarded from contact with people who are considered unsuitable because the person presents a risk to their safety or welfare. Our criminal law,[2] our public family law and our administrative law must respond to the necessity of placing a child's safety and welfare as the paramount consideration. Teachers and social workers and others who work with children must face the prospect that they will be barred from working in their chosen profession as a result of behaviour by them in relation to children in their care that places these children at risk.

---

[1]   Protection of Children Act 1999; Care Standards Act 2000; Education (Restriction of Employment) Regulations 2000 (S.I. 2000 No. 2419).

[2]   This paper is not concerned with the criminal law, where a court can disqualify a person from working with children and young persons as part of the sentence after a criminal conviction. See Criminal Justice and Court Services Act 2000 ss. 26-42. The Care Standards Tribunal will receive review applications from people in this position but only 10 years after sentence (5 years in the case of a person under 18 at the time of sentence).

Inevitably, however, there are major and sometimes conflicting policy issues. For example, should safeguarding children extend to protecting them from the behaviour in private of an adult whose example may be 'unacceptable'.[3] And what amounts to 'unacceptable'? It is not possible to provide a comprehensive definition, and the Guidance for Education Staff goes no further than referring to 'behaviour, which involves a breach of a teacher's position of trust, or a breach of the standards of propriety, expected of the profession'.[4]

England and Wales has struggled with these dilemmas throughout most of the last fifty years. It has to be said that the difficulties may well have been increased by the need to ensure a balanced service for vulnerable children that encourages 'efforts to work alongside families rather than disempower them'. Thus the focus has been on the overall needs of children rather than the narrow concentration on an alleged incident.[5] Inevitably, the requirement to support families in a non-threatening way has resulted occasionally in individual failures and sadly sometimes also in institutional failures to protect children. A failure by a professional requires the availability of emergency powers to remove the professional from his or her position of trust.

But we are talking here of draconian powers. The implementation of the Human Rights Act 1998, bringing European Convention standards into direct application in the domestic law, has highlighted the tension that has always existed between children's welfare on the one hand and the right to work as a professional or a volunteer in a chosen child centred profession.[6]

Principles of proportionality, so important in any consideration of the European Convention on Human Rights, must now play the critical role in these difficult and sensitive decisions, for there are two conflicting arguments, both clearly understandable, that can be persuasive.

First, it could be argued that the creation of a system that bars a person from working with children in certain situations is necessary so as to instil confidence in the provision both of public child care and the educational services. The ultimate justification is the protection of children from the risk of harm; thus balance and proportionality in an individual case are not the only factors. There may be a trump card.

Secondly, and in contrast, some may argue that in the context of these essentially individual decisions taken by the Government departments is the sometimes overriding need of Government to ensure that the crisis in teacher and social work numbers is not unduly accentuated. Another not wholly unconnected

---

3   See for example paragraph 25 of the guidance document produced by the Department for Education and Skills entitled *Preventing Unsuitable People from Working with Children and Young Persons* (Revised November 2001).
4   Paragraph 19(c).
5   *Child Protection – Messages from Research* (1995) London HMSO.
6   See the decision of the Registered Homes Tribunal (No. 420) where an individual who ran a residential care home was acquitted of sexual abuse allegations yet had his registration of the home cancelled. His appeal to the Registered Homes Tribunal was dismissed. The decision is available on the Department of Health Website.

policy concern relates to the growing number of residential homes that become uneconomic and therefore must otherwise close because they cannot meet the exacting demands imposed upon them by the newly created National Care Standards Commission policy.[7] These are matters that cannot be wholly ignored by decision makers, either at first instance or on appeal.

In weighing these policy issues, it is argued here that proportionality and balance must be a key link to ensure that the correct approach is taken and thus that possibly conflicting policy considerations are placed in the appropriate balance. Indeed, case law prior to the introduction of statutory safeguards, when only a non-statutory framework was in place, gave balance a central position. Thus In *R v. Secretary of State for Health, ex parte C*,[8] Hale L.J. said:

> Underlying this issue is the balance to be struck between two important interests. One is the interest of any individual in safeguarding his reputation and livelihood against the serious interference which inclusion on anything like an official 'blacklist' may entail. The other is the interest of children living away from home, and the interest of the community which seeks to safeguard its vulnerable members, in effective protection from abuse and neglect and other risks to which they are subject ...

Newman J, in *R v. Worcester County Council, Secretary of State for the Department of Health, ex parte 'S.W.'*[9] said much the same. The Judge in that case said:

> Assuming as I do that the consequences of being included on the index is to interfere with employment, I see no ground for concluding that the index[10] is ... disproportionate to the objective to be obtained.

---

[7] *The Times* Newspaper for July 2, 2002 reported the sad story at the other end of life, of a lady aged 108 who was moved to a new care home when her home had to close because it was unable to meet the more exacting standards of the Care Standards Act 2000. This was obviously a traumatic move for a lady of this advanced age and she died within a month, apparently after refusing food in her new home.

[8] [2000] EWCA 49. This particular case did not conclude at that stage. The case before the Court of Appeal concerned a review of the decision to place C on the then non-statutory 'consultancy' index maintained by the Department. His name was transferred on to the statutory list when the Protection of Children Act 1999 came into force. An appeal was heard by the Tribunal and his appeal was allowed [0037]. The Department appealed on a point of law to the High Court, and the appeal was heard by Scott Baker J. in early June 2002. The appeal was dismissed (*C v. Secretary of State for Health*) [2002] EWCH 1381 (Admin). See further footnote 25.

[9] [2000] EWHC Admin 392. 'SW' took matters further when the Tribunal came into existence. The Tribunal dismissed his appeal after a hearing in April 2002. [2002.4.PC].

[10] The former non-statutory list maintained by the Department of Health.

In *Secretary of State for Health v. C*,[11] Scott Baker J. refers to the listing under the statutory scheme as involving a difficult balancing exercise between the safety of children and the rights of individuals to have their livelihoods and reputations safeguarded.

The new Tribunal and policy considerations

The Care Standards Tribunal came into existence in England and Wales from April 1, 2002. It incorporates two existing Tribunals, the old Registered Homes Tribunal and the newly created Protection of Children Act Tribunal. It has been given wider powers as a result of the Care Standards Act 2000.

The purpose of this paper is to consider the human rights issues that are raised by this new jurisdiction. It is true to say that the Act itself is a response in a sense to the Human Rights Act 1998, in the need to ensure that administrative decision making is compliant with the European Convention. All Government departments audited their procedures in the light of the implementation and it was concluded that the procedures barring individuals from working with children were wanting. The creation of the Protection of Children Act Tribunal introduces an independent tier of merits review of administrative decisions in this field.[12] It was felt that judicial review of administrative action was not sufficient to comply with the Convention provisions, in particular, Article 6. Whether this approach was unduly cautious is of little consequence any more. In any event, judicial pronouncements in the analogous field of housing law suggest that compliance based on judicial review alone cannot be taken as read. Laws L.J. in *Runa Begum v. Tower Hamlets L.B.C.*[13] set out a framework for analysing when administrative schemes might or might not be compliant. At one end of the paradigm would be those cases where a scheme's subject matter involved the resolution of primary fact, whilst at the other end would be those cases where the subject matter generally or systematically required the application of judgment or the exercise of discretion, especially if it involved the weighing of policy issues and regard being had to the interests of others who were not before the decision maker. According to Laws L.J.'s approach, in the latter situation the court would be satisfied, for the purposes of Article 6, with a form of inquisition at first instance in which the decision-maker was more of an expert than a judge, and the second instance appeal was in the nature of judicial review. In contrast, in the former situation, involving fact finding, a judicial review jurisdiction might not suffice. Where within the spectrum would fall decisions taken by the Department of Health, Department of Education and

---

11   [2002] EWHC 1381 (Admin).
12   Protection of Children Act 1999 s.9.   Schedule 1 of the Act sets out the
          constitution of the Tribunal. Each appeal has a legally qualified Chairman and two
          lay members. The lay members are appointed by the President of the Tribunal
          from amongst the lay panel established by reference to the expertise set out in
          Regulation 3 of the Protection of Children and Vulnerable Adults and Care
          Standards Tribunal Regulations 2002 (S.I. 2002 No. 816).
13   [2002] 2 All E.R. 668.

Skills, or the now created National Care Standards Commission, in relation to preventing individuals or organisations from working with children, can only be open to conjecture. There is certainly fact finding required for all decisions in this area, and thus it is likely that Article 6 considerations would demand a full merits appeal of the decision.

One final matter of policy requires a mention. The jurisdiction of the Tribunal has been established to provide a merits appeal of decisions, for example, to place individuals on the statutory lists barring them from working with children or to cancel registration of proprietors of care homes. There is no merits appeal for relatives and others who, having complained of the conduct of particular individuals, find that the complaint does not result in a barring decision. It could be argued that the absence of any appeal in this situation sends an unfortunate message to those who expect an even-handed approach to child protection issues. The relatives faced with a rejection of their complaints against particular individuals have no satisfactory remedy at the present time.

The case law of the Tribunal

There is an important statutory difference between the social work cases and the education cases. In the case of social workers, there is a two fold test laid down by Statute, namely, misconduct and unsuitability. In the education cases, it is not necessary as such to have to prove unsuitability to work with children.[14] Misconduct, medical reasons, or that 'he is not a fit and proper person to be employed as a teacher' will do, and it is implied that the teacher is unsuitable if one of these grounds is made out.

We consider first some of the social work cases that have been decided by the Tribunal. The Tribunal's powers in relation to social workers who are placed on the list as being unsuitable to work with children are contained in s.4(3) of the Protection of Children Act 1999 as amended by s.99 of the Care Standards Act 2000. The section reads as follows:

> If on an appeal or determination under this section the Tribunal is not satisfied of either of the following, namely – (a) that the individual was guilty of misconduct (whether or not in the course of his duties) which harmed the child or placed the child at risk of harm; and (b) that the individual is unsuitable to work with children, the Tribunal shall allow the appeal or determine the issue in the

---

14   This was accepted by the Tribunal in the education case of *M v. Secretary of State for Education and Skills* [2002.11.PC] where the Tribunal decided that M had downloaded child pornography on to his home computer, but where there was no suggestion that he had misbehaved in any way in school. He had been convicted by a Magistrates' Court of a criminal offence but the conviction had been set aside by the Crown Court. The Tribunal of course applied a 'balance of probability' test rather than a 'beyond reasonable doubt' test, and the Tribunal had before it more evidence of the material than the material that had formed the basis of the criminal procedure.

individual's favour and (in either case) direct his removal from the list; otherwise
it shall dismiss the appeal or direct the individual's inclusion in the list.

The burden of proof is on the Secretary of State, the standard of proof being the
civil standard of a balance of probability. The Tribunal has followed the approach
of Lord Nicholls in the child care case, *Re H and Others*[15] where he said:

> Where the matters in issue are facts, the standard of proof required in non-criminal
> proceedings is the preponderance of probability, usually referred to as the balance
> of probability ...
> When assessing the probabilities the court will have in mind as a factor, to
> whatever extent is appropriate in the particular case, that the more serious the
> allegation the less likely it is that the event occurred and, hence, the stronger
> should be the evidence before the court concludes that the allegation is established
> on the balance of probability.

Lord Hoffman said much the same in a national security case, *Secretary of State
for the Home Department v. Rehman*[16]

> It would need more cogent evidence to satisfy one that the creature seen walking
> in Regent's Park was more likely than not to have been a lioness than to be
> satisfied to the same standard of probability that it was an Alsatian. In this basis,
> cogent evidence is generally required to satisfy a civil tribunal that a person has ...
> behaved in some ... reprehensible manner.

An interesting case that illustrates the human rights perspective of the
jurisdiction of the Tribunal is *Barnes v. Secretary of State for Health*.[17] The facts of
this case relate to events that occurred in children's homes managed by the former
Clwyd and Gwynedd County Councils in North Wales in the 1970s and 1980s. A
major police investigation had begun in 1991, and this resulted in a number of
residential social workers being convicted of serious sexual and physical abuse.
Other social workers, although not prosecuted, were also named in the major report
into the abuse of children who had been placed in residential care homes in these
areas ('*Lost in Care*': the *Waterhouse Inquiry*).[18] One of these was Mr Barnes, and
thus on January 4, 2001, the Department wrote to Mr Barnes informing him that
his name was being included in the statutory list barring him from working with
children. A flavour of the approach taken by the Waterhouse Inquiry in relation to
Mr Barnes is the following:

15   [1996] 1 All E.R. 1 at p.16.
16   [2002] 1 All E.R. 122 at p.141.
17   [0070] All the Tribunal decisions will be available on the Tribunal website,
      www.carestandardstribunal.gov.uk. This case is reproduced in Pearl and
      Hershman, *Care Standards Legislation Handbook*, (Jordans) (2002).
18   HC 201. HMSO, (2000). The Report runs to 937 pages. It concluded that
      widespread sexual abuse of boys and physical abuse in the sense of unacceptable
      use of force in disciplining and restraining residents occurred in children's
      residential homes in Clwyd and Gwynedd between 1974 and 1990. It made 72
      recommendations.

...we are satisfied that Barnes was viewed by some of the residents as a remote, unfriendly and arrogant figure and that he was responsible for instituting, or at least maintaining, what they saw as an oppressive and authoritarian regime ...[19]

The Department identified nine particular instances of misconduct. Of these nine, the Tribunal was satisfied that he harmed a child or placed a child at risk of harm on two of these occasions. The Tribunal then went on to consider whether, in consequence of these two findings, Mr Barnes was unsuitable to work with children. The Tribunal said as follows:

> There will of course be cases where it necessarily follows that a finding of misconduct carries with it the inevitable finding of unsuitability. There will be other cases where a finding of misconduct does not carry with it this consequence ... It must be said that context, in this situation, is very important indeed. We have found proved two allegations of excessive discipline that occurred more than twenty years ago. Mr Barnes had responsibility, on any showing, for some very disturbed youngsters ... We have placed in the balance our findings as to misconduct, when they happened and the context in which they occurred, as against his career as a social worker extending over many years ... It is our view that the Protection of Children Act 1999 obliges us to adopt a proportionate response to our findings of misconduct. In this case, having heard all that has been said on behalf of Mr Barnes, and taking into account the two findings of misconduct, we are not satisfied on a balance of probability that Mr Barnes is unsuitable to work with children.

The appeal was therefore allowed and the Department was directed to remove his name from the list. In an earlier case, *Hall v. Secretary of State for Health*,[20] the allegations were of a serious sexual nature and the Tribunal concluded that the allegations, if proved, were of such seriousness that it would be a clear indication that he is unsuitable to work with children. In the result, in that case, the allegations were proved, and in consequence the appeal was dismissed.

A second case arising out of the events in North Wales is *Joan Glover v. Secretary of State for Health*.[21] Mrs Glover was found by the Inquiry, and the Tribunal, to have physically assaulted a number of children in her care. She admitted that 'she used a slap as a last resort' across the legs or the bottom. Once she slapped a child across the face. On the basis of these admissions, the Tribunal had no difficulty in making findings of misconduct that harmed a child or placed a child at risk of harm. As to unsuitability today, the Tribunal said:

> The Tribunal accepted that it does not follow that the applicant remains unsuitable to work with children in 2002 simply because she was unsuitable to work with children in 1979 or 1981. However, defects of character and temperament are not easily changed and do not usually change unless they are specifically addressed. There was no evidence that the applicant had taken any steps to confront or to modify her character or temperament.

---

[19]   '*Lost in Care*', para 13.56.
[20]   [0003].
[21]   [0077].

The appeal was dismissed.

Woodcock v. Secretary of State for Health[22] is another case that raised issues based on allegations going back many years, in this case between 1987 and 1992. As in other cases, a substantial volume of written and video evidence had by now been lost or destroyed. The allegations against him related to inappropriate sexual touching of young boys in his care. The Tribunal was satisfied as to the most serious of these allegations. It went on to say:

> Given the seriousness of the allegations which we have found proved, we have no doubt that Mr Woodcock is unsuitable to work with children. We reached this conclusion both because of the seriousness of the misconduct and the fact that Mr Woodcock has consistently denied that misconduct and has hence no opportunity for treatment which might have led us to a different conclusion.[23]

Evidence in these cases is always difficult to produce, and there are two cases that both illustrate the point. *C v. Secretary of State for Health*[24] related to allegations of rape by a foster parent back in 1983, and certain allegations that his own children and step-children had been mistreated by him when they were young. The police and the Crown Prosecution Service investigated a late complaint, but no further action was taken. C was however placed on the list barring him from working with children and young persons. The Tribunal referred to the fact that in considering C's appeal against the decision to bar him from working with children, C was 'entitled to a fair hearing by an independent and impartial tribunal established by law'. The allegations could not be tested by live evidence, because the person who made the allegation was not called to give evidence. The Tribunal allowed the appeal, stating:

> Findings can only be based on evidence and we must not speculate. That would be unfair to all those involved ... The evidence that he is guilty of misconduct is simply not there.

The Secretary of State appealed and his appeal was dismissed.[25] The Administrative Court said that the Tribunal was right to have allowed C's appeal and there had been no error of law on the part of the Tribunal. The court said that it would be slow to interfere with the decision of a Tribunal 'composed of particular members selected for their expertise'. The issues faced by the Tribunal had been issues of fact that the Tribunal had been in the best position to decide.

---

22   2002.4. P.C.
23   A similar approach was taken in *Jackson* [0061], where Mr Jackson had been acquitted of sexual assault. The Tribunal, applying a balance of probability test rather than the criminal test of beyond reasonable doubt, decided that it was more likely than not that he was guilty of the sexual assault, and that he was in consequence unsuitable to work with children.
24   [0037]. This case is reported in Family Law, July [2002] 515 with a comment by Professor Gillian Douglas.
25   [2002] EWHC 1381 (Admin).

A similar result to that in *C*, although for differing reasons, occurred in *Black v. Secretary of State for Health*.[26] Allegations were made by 'A' that back in the 1980s, whilst in residential care, he had been sexually abused by Mr Black. The disclosure was made in 1998. As with most of these cases, no criminal prosecution took place. Nevertheless, Mr Black was eventually placed on the list as a person who was unsuitable to work with children. He appealed. The Tribunal heard a great deal of live evidence in this case,[27] in contrast to that in *C* where no live evidence was presented. The Tribunal looked in particular at the circumstances surrounding the disclosure and the conflicting evidence that was presented about 'A's' truthfulness. In the final analysis, they concluded that his evidence was unreliable, and in consequence the appeal was allowed.

Those are two cases where findings of fact went in favour of the appellant. If the findings of fact go against the appellant, the Tribunal must turn its attention to unsuitability. Here, the Tribunal must assess risk and inevitably a failure to undergo treatment to address the various concerns is an important and possibly overwhelming factor. Thus in *Miles v. Secretary of State for Health*,[28] yet another case concerning excessive discipline of children in residential care a number of years ago, the Tribunal suggested that the evidential burden was on the applicant to show suitability:

> ... the fact of the matter was that Mr Miles had not undergone any treatment of any kind to address the issue and without some psychiatric or medical evidence to show that Mr Miles was no longer a risk to children, the Tribunal could not find that Mr Miles was now suitable to work with children.[29]

A similar approach was taken in *Glover*[30] where the Tribunal, in dealing with a lack of any supporting statements for Mrs Glover, said:

> The burden was not upon the applicant to establish her suitability. The legal burden remained upon the Secretary of State to establish unsuitability. However, having been found, in terms, to have been unsuitable to work with children in the past, the applicant did have some obligation to adduce positive evidence of change or difference, from professional colleagues or supervisors. The tribunal was troubled by her failure to do so.

---

[26]   [0087].
[27]   'A' was deemed to be a 'vulnerable adult' and his evidence, in accordance with the Rules, was given by live video link.
[28]   [0047].
[29]   In *Swindells v. Secretary of State for Health* [0042], the applicant had been in weekly therapy for three years, but there was no information regarding the results of the therapy, and thus the Tribunal was unable to satisfy itself that the applicant, convicted in Germany of distributing child pornography, no longer posed a risk of re-offending. In *Woodcock* [2002.4.PC], the Tribunal referred to the fact that Mr Woodcock had consistently denied the misconduct and 'hence had no opportunity for treatment which might have led us to a different conclusion (on unsuitability)'.
[30]   [0077].

We turn briefly to look at two of the education cases. In *Mason v. Secretary of State for Education and Skills*,[31] Mr Mason had formed a consensual sexual relationship with a 16-year-old former pupil. The relationship began during the summer holidays after the pupil had left the school. In the autumn, with the relationship still continuing, she went to a senior school that shared the same site and had the same headmaster. The Tribunal decided that his name should remain on the list and his employment restricted. The Tribunal said:

> We have no doubt that Mr Mason now realises that he made a serious error of judgment in his relationship with pupil X. However, we are not convinced that Mr Mason has yet developed the maturity to understand fully why boundaries should be set and how and where to obtain appropriate advice should difficulties occur.[32]

The education area is different from the social work field in that a teacher can be placed on the list for medical reasons. The Guidance refers to medical conditions such as drug or alcohol abuse or mental illness that significantly impairs his or her abilities to discharge their responsibilities as a teacher.[33] The only case so far where an appeal has been heard after a person has been placed on the list for medical reasons is *MacBride v. Secretary of State for Education and Skills*[34] where the medical evidence suggested chronic anxiety symptoms, both generalised and specific. The Tribunal formed the view on the basis of the evidence before it that the medical condition of this teacher was such that the welfare of children being taught by her was likely to be at risk. It therefore dismissed the appeal.

Conclusions

The Care Standards Act 2000 is a wide ranging statute. It establishes a new independent regulatory body for social care and private and voluntary health care in England, the National Care Standards Commission. In Wales, these services are now under the control of the National Assembly for Wales. An independent Council has also been established to register social workers and to set standards in social work. An independent Children's Commissioner has been established in Wales, and it may well be that a similar scheme will be introduced in time in England as well. Childminders and day care providers are now also regulated.

---

31   [0078].
32   See also, the case concerning downloading of child pornography (*M v. Secretary of State for Education and Skills* [2002.11.PC]) where, having found the allegation proved, the Tribunal dismissed the appeal. A slightly different result was reached in *X v Secretary of State for Education and Skills* [0065] where the Tribunal in effect laid down certain conditions that should be applied to the appellant who had written obscene messages on his window in the school house where he lived about girls he was teaching.
33   *Preventing Unsuitable People from Working with Children and Young Persons* (Revised November 2001).
34   [0080]. This case is reproduced in Pearl and Hershman, *Care Standards Legislation Handbook* (Jordans, 2002).

There is an expanded statutory list of those unsuitable to work with vulnerable adults. Appeals in these areas are brought before the Care Standards Tribunal.

It is likely, in the light of ongoing reforms of the administrative justice system in England and Wales, that the specialist education and health Tribunals will draw closer together. These early decisions will provide a framework for the developments in the future, maintaining the central policy that the safety and welfare of our children must be protected, whilst at the same time ensuring that an individual's human rights are not ignored whenever decisions are taken to prohibit people from working with children and young people. The early history of the Care Standards Tribunal makes clear that decisions of Government Ministers are not simply 'rubber stamped'. Although the decisions of the Tribunal are of course individual decisions on particular facts, the indications are that it has begun to lay down guidance that will help in the formulation of standards in this sensitive area of social policy.

Chapter 7

When Cultures Clash:
Aborigines and Inheritance in Australia

Prue Vines

Introduction

The statutory and common law regimes of inheritance law which apply to Aboriginal people and Torres Strait Islanders in Australia rest on a number of myths. Calling them myths both suggests their power in the community and reflects their uncertain relation to truth as it can be ascertained from the evidence.

In this chapter I set out the myths and then the more accurate picture which can be ascertained from the available evidence. I then examine the impact those myths have had on the way statutory and common law (English-derived) regimes have been developed and applied. The regimes are outlined, with particular emphasis on those which have been developed to apply to 'traditional' Aborigines. Some of these hold themselves out as recognising customary law. I argue that there are significant problems with all the regimes which apply to Aboriginal people on intestacy. Some legislative action might be remedial, but there is a strong argument for making dedicated legal aid funds available to make wills for Aboriginal people, not as a method of allowing individuals to have their free will, but to allow for expression of customary law.

Challenging the myths

Myth No.1: Aboriginal people in Australia are either traditional or non-traditional

This myth, that Aboriginal people live purely traditional or purely westernised lives, has significant force in Australia. Part of the reason for this is that Australia is so highly urbanised and the proportion of Aboriginal people in Australia is so small (1.1% in 1986, possibly 1.5% in 1996) that few non-Aboriginal Australians are aware of their presence except where strong media coverage exists. Media coverage tends to emphasise simplistic divisions of Aborigines into traditional or non-traditional, and the small population proportions do not give enough people the opportunity to recognise the falsity of the division. The pattern of populations of rural and urban Aborigines from the 1986 census emphasises rural Aboriginal populations in Western Australia, Northern Territory and Queensland and more urban Aboriginal populations in NSW and Victoria.[1] In most States about one-third of the Aboriginal population was located in rural areas, although the proportion in the Northern Territory was very much higher. This pattern was confirmed by data in 1991 which showed that '28% of the Aboriginal and Torres Strait Islander population lived in capital cities and just under 20% in rural and remote [i.e. remote rural] areas with 50% in towns and rural localities [rural towns and surrounding areas]'.[2] The data for the 1996 census is similar.[3]

All this evidence is taken from censuses. It is therefore a snapshot of where the population was situated at one time. It is easy to assume that this static statistical picture reflects people making lifetime choices. The evidence shows, however, that Aboriginal people have a more complex relationship between traditional and urban lifestyles. Research done for the Royal Commission into Aboriginal Deaths in Custody showed that: [4]

> [D]efinite age-gender patterns exist in these population movements. The people moving out tend to be older people and their young children. This suggests that the stereotypes of the 'urban Aboriginal person' and the 'rural Aboriginal person', frequently used by non-Aboriginal commentators, may have little factual basis. Over much of Australia we are perhaps seeing an Aboriginal population that is quite mobile, with its members moving between the cities and the country at different stages in their lives.

Aboriginal people, then, move backwards and forwards between city and country, and indeed between relatively traditional and non-traditional lifestyles within each person's lifetime. Thus their culture and understanding of themselves and their relationships with others remains relatively constant, and cannot be sensibly divided into 'rural' or 'traditional' and 'urban'. In particular, ideas about kinship and the law continue to be reinforced wherever Aboriginal people live, with possibly greater emphasis when in rural areas.

Myth No.2: Traditional Aboriginal people are all part of the same culture

This myth is gradually giving way to education about the diversity of Aboriginal groups and cultures. However, it is still having an impact. Evidence of the diversity of Aboriginal groups and cultures begins with acknowledging the multiplicity of language groups. In 1788 there were probably up to 600 language groups in

---

[1]   E. Johnston, Royal Commission into *Aboriginal Deaths in Custody, National Report,* Volume 1, Australian Government Publishing Service (1991), p 37.

[2]   Australian Bureau of Statistics *Census of Population and Housing, 6 August 1991, Australia's Aboriginal and Torres Strait Islander Population,* A.G.P.S., Canberra (1993) at p.2.

[3]   Australian Bureau of Statistics, Occasional Paper: *Population Issues – Aboriginal and Torres Strait Islander Population,* A.B.S. (2001).

[4]   E. Johnston, *Royal Commission into Aboriginal Deaths in Custody, National Report,* Volume 1, Australian Government Publishing Service (1991), p.39. This refers to work reported by A Gray, *Aboriginal Migration to the Cities* (1989) 6 (2) Journal of the Australian Population Association 122-44.

existence in Australia.[5] Anthropological studies have shown wide diversity in
kinship structures and obligations and in ways of life. However there are some
central matters on which there is agreement amongst most Aboriginal groups –
such as, for example, the idea that religion is the basis for law and that kinship is
vital for prescribing behaviour.[6]

*Myth No.3: Aboriginal people with urban lifestyles have the same ideas about
family and culture as non-Aboriginal people with urban lifestyles*

This is related to the second myth. One of the major differences between the two
groups is the secular nature of non-Aboriginal culture in Australia and the strong
sense of the sacred in Aboriginal culture.[7] Australian society in general is
extremely secular. There is no established Church and no formal separation of
church and state either. In this way it differs from both England and the United
States. Censuses no longer require people to state their religion, but in the last one
to do so, 1981, 20% of people said they had no religion or did not answer.[8] By
1996 this figure had grown to 25.6%.[9] However Aboriginal society is recognised
as one where law and religion intertwine to such an extent that it may not be
possible to differentiate between them.[10] However, most Australians assume that if
an Aboriginal family is living an urban life, that they have lost their cultural base,
and have become no longer 'authentically' Aboriginal. The contrary appears to be
true. As Eversley[11] observed of urban Aborigines in south-west Western Australia:

> ... A Noongar child is taught to regard an aunt as a mother and her cousins as her
> sisters and her brothers. The classificatory kinship system apparent in more
> traditional communities ... is still strongly apparent ... this communalised method
> of child-rearing is the very core of Noongar social structure and organisation ...

5   G. Blainey, *A Land Half Won*, Macmillan, Melbourne (1980); R. M. and C. H.
     Berndt, *The World of the First Australians*, Ure Smith, Sydney (1977); K.
     Maddock, *The Australian Aborigines*, Allen Lane, London (1975).
6   R. M. and C. H Berndt, *The World of the First Australians*, Ure Smith, Sydney
     (1977).
7   See P. Vines, *Bodily Remains in the Cemetery and the Burial Ground; A
     Comparative Anthropology of Law and Death or How Long can I stay?* in
     Manderson D. (ed), *Courting Death*, Pluto Press, London (1999).
8   H. Mol, *The Faith of Australians* (1985) at p.6.
9   Australian Bureau of Statistics, *Australia Now: Population – Religion*,
     www.abs.gov/ausstats/abs, 4.12.2001.
10   See for example, W. E. H. Stanner, *'The Dreaming'* in W.H. Edwards (ed)
     Traditional Aboriginal Society, Macmillan, Melbourne (1987).
11   R. Eversley, *The South-West Aboriginal and Family Law*, No 11, *Family Law*,
     Institute of Family Studies, Melbourne (1984) quoted in McRae, Nettheim and
     Beacroft *Indigenous Legal Issues*, 2nd ed., L.B.C. (1997).

Myth No.4: Aboriginal people are not interested in property or inheritance

This (sometimes convenient) myth seems to arise amongst people who have a view of Aborigines as the ultimate communitarians. The Aboriginal community has worked hard to teach non-Aboriginals the singular importance of Aboriginals' relationship to land. Unfortunately this knowledge that the relationship between land and Aboriginal is different from that of non-Aboriginal people and land has at times been translated into the view that ownership does not matter to Aboriginal people. This is a profound misunderstanding of Aboriginal views of obligations and tradition.

The non-Aboriginal view of ownership of land as expressed in the common law was and is a highly secular view. The usable nature of land was paramount - land was seen as a commodity, and the ownership of land was commodifiable. In *Milirrpum v Nabalco*, Blackburn J recognised the differences (while feeling unable to decide to protect the Aboriginal form of ownership) when he held:

> I think that property ... generally implies the right to use or enjoy, the right to exclude others, and the right to alienate ... . [B]y this standard I do not think that I can characterize the relationship of the clan to the land as proprietary.
>
> ... The greatest extent to which it is true that the clan as such has the right to use and enjoy the clan territory is that the clan may, in a sense in which other clans may not ... perform ritual ceremonies on the land. That the clan has a duty to the land – to care for it – is another matter. This is not without parallels in our law... . But this resemblance is not, or at any rate is only in a very slight degree, an indication of a proprietary interest.[12]

Mabo (No 2)[13] was important in relation to this point in that it recognised native title as a proprietary title which did not have to partake of this commodity approach because its roots lay outside the common law. *Mabo* recognised that custodial property could be recognised by common law.

There are a number of problems with the myth that Aboriginal people are not concerned about property and therefore about inheritance. This myth only applies to property as a commodity. The custodial view of property turns this on its head – and inheritance therefore also includes inheritance of custodianship. This is quite clear when we consider the way Aboriginal people feel about burial sites and burial grounds and the need for the recognition of this aspect of cultural heritage.[14] This

12   *Milirrpum v Nabalco Pty Ltd and the Commonwealth of Australia* [1971] 17 F.L.R. 141 at p.272.
13   *Mabo v Queensland (No 2)* (1992) 175 C.L.R. 1. This case decided finally that the doctrine of *terra nullius* (land belonging to no-one) was a legal fiction in its application to Australia, and that native title to land could be recognised by the common law of Australia.
14   Legislation exists in all Australian jurisdictions to deal with this issue. The Commonwealth legislation is the Aboriginal and Torres Strait Islander Heritage Protection Act (Cth.) 1984. See P. Vines, *Resting in Peace: A Comparison of the Legal Control of Bodily Remains in Cemeteries and Aboriginal Burial Grounds in Australia* (1998) 20 (1) Sydney Law Review 78.

attitude to ownership may also apply to chattels or objects of ritual significance. This aspect of inheritance is essential for people to continue their obligations of custodianship, but it is not addressed in any of the intestacy legislation in Australia, whether it pays lip-service to customary law or otherwise.

Inheritance of native title land is normally unproblematic because it is held by a group. However, a considerable portion of non-native title land is owned by Aborigines, either bought using Land Funds,[15] or in some other way,[16] so land may still be an issue of inheritance. An Aboriginal person may well purchase some land in fee simple in a country town or city during the period in their life when they are pursuing urban things, and it may therefore need to be passed on that person's death.

What of other property?[17] The inheritance of intellectual property including ritual knowledge and artwork is a very important matter in Aboriginal communities. This itself is a matter of customary law because artwork or medicinal knowledge may be derived from community knowledge or ritual. Passing on obligations relating to ritual knowledge is an important issue of custodial property. Obligations arising from kinship to care for children or other members of the community also need to be addressed.

Myth No.5: Aboriginal people are defined by blood

The predominant way others have defined Aboriginal people in Australia since 1788 has been by blood. Colonial legislation referred to 'Aboriginal natives of New South Wales and New Holland' and later State and Commonwealth legislation frequently followed this practice, using 'Aboriginal natives of Australia' or 'Aboriginal Natives of New South Wales [or other state or territory]'.[18] Legislative definitions also referred to 'half-caste', 'full-blood' etc, but depending on the purpose of the act could refer to 'any descendant'. For example, the Western Australian Aboriginal Affairs Planning Authority Act defines Aboriginality as

---

15   For example, the N.S.W. Aboriginal Land Fund – the Aboriginal Land Rights Act 1983 (N.S.W.) set up Land Councils (representative Aboriginal groups) who could claim (rarely) or buy land with the funds derived from land tax. 7.5% of all State Land Tax raised between 1984 and 1998 was put into the land fund to provide an interest-earning investment with an income that could be used to buy land. This was particularly important in N.S.W. which is the most settled State of Australia and has the highest proportion of dispossessed Aboriginal people. The Indigenous Land Corporation (Commonwealth body) now does most land-purchasing Australia wide.
16   For example, trusts: Aboriginal Land Trusts Act 1966 (S.A.); Aboriginal Land Act 1991 (Qld.); Torres Strait Islander Act 1991 (Qld.); Victoria: for political reasons the legislation in Victoria is partly Commonwealth legislation: Aboriginal Land Act 1987 (Cth.), Land Act 1991 (Vic.).
17   See T. Janke, *Our Culture, Our Future; proposals for recognition and protection of Indigenous Cultural and Intellectual Property*, Australian Institute of Aboriginal Studies, Canberra (1997).
18   J. McCorquodale, *Aboriginal Identity: Legislative, Judicial and Administrative Definitions* (1997) No 2 Australian Aboriginal Studies 24-35 at pp.25-26.

requiring at least one-quarter Aboriginal blood. Other definitions used have relied on the idea that customary law marriage is a definitive indicator of Aboriginality.

The usual way of defining Aboriginal people in Australia for most purposes is now a person of Aboriginal descent (no degree of descent required) who identifies themselves and is identified by the Aboriginal community as Aboriginal. There is some question of whether descent is required at all.[19]

After-death rituals and distribution of property

In Aboriginal culture

When a person dies in Aboriginal culture, a number of things may happen. There are various rituals to be carried out because the spirit has become separated from the body. Much of the deceased's property may be disposed of with the body – belongings may be burnt. In most groups the place where the deceased lived would be destroyed and the rest of the family would move away. Customary law changes over time. Now that many people live in permanent houses, some customs have changed – people are less likely to destroy things that belonged to the deceased. Similarly houses are unlikely to be destroyed, but it is common for the family of the deceased to move out for several months or swap with other distant relatives for the period of mourning. The deceased person will have had kinship obligations which need to be dealt with, and they will have owned sacred objects for which customary law will determine the inheritance. Personal possessions will pass according to customary law, which may well be secret. Kinship obligations will arise whether a person is living a traditional or urban lifestyle, and those obligations may be met with non-traditional property.

The general framework of legal regulation of inheritance in Australia

Non-Aboriginal culture in Australia also carried out rituals after death, but property is distributed according to the statutory and common law of inheritance or succession.

Australian succession law is a common law system which emphasises the importance of wills. The system is complicated by the fact that there are eight legal regimes (one for each of the states and two territories),[20] all of which have different laws of inheritance, although the differences between them tend to be of detail. The dominant paradigm is the paradigm of testamentary freedom and the testator is regarded as able to deal with his or her property as he or she wishes. All the

---

[19]   *Attorney-General (Cth) v Qld; National Aboriginal and Islander Legal Services Secretariat v Queensland* (1990) 94 A.L.R. 515.

[20]   These are the six states (New South Wales, Victoria, South Australia, Queensland, Western Australia, Tasmania) and the two territories (Australian Capital Territory and Northern Territory). The Commonwealth of Australia is the ninth jurisdiction, but it does not have a succession jurisdiction.

jurisdictions have intestacy legislation[21] which determines who will take what if there is no will. The general scheme of the intestacy legislation is to give primacy to the spouse (one spouse only, including *de facto*, and, in some places, homosexual partner) and issue of the deceased. If only a spouse survives and no issue, there are two models – everything to the spouse (in New South Wales, Victoria, Tasmania, South Australia, and the Australian Capital Territory) or the spouse shares with relatives (in Queensland, Western Australia and the Northern Territory). If neither spouse nor issue exists, the property goes to relatives in order: parents, siblings, grandparents, uncles and aunts, next of kin according to civil law (in Tasmania and Victoria only), and then to the Crown in *bona vacantia*. The presence of relatives in any of these classes will preclude later classes.

All the jurisdictions also have Family Provision regimes.[22] These are of interest because they provide for a select group of people to challenge the will or intestacy on the basis of inadequate provision. The people entitled to challenge are first, spouse and children, and then in different jurisdictions, some other people. New South Wales has probably the broadest group: in the category of spouse it includes husband/ wife; *de facto* husband/wife; homosexual partner, and (although with extra hurdles) former spouse. In the category of child is included legitimate, illegitimate and adopted children and children of 'a domestic relationship' – that is a 'close personal relationship between two adult persons who ... are living together, one or each of whom provides the other with domestic support and personal care.' People outside these categories are eligible in New South Wales if they were ever dependent on the deceased and were either a grandchild or a member of the deceased's household.

Narrower family provision regimes such as that of Queensland require dependency of any person other than spouse and children in order to be eligible to challenge the provision made by the will.

Defining kin

The definition of family in general Australian culture

What is notable about the legislation is its dependence on the ideas of lineal family relationships and relationships of blood rather than collateral relationships. This is characteristic of the 'western world's' general treatment of kinship. It tends to be lineal, indeed patrilineal, and to emphasise blood relationship over other

21   Administration and Probate Act (A. & P.) 1929 Pt III (A.C.T.); Wills Probate and Administration Act (W.P.A.) 1898 Pt II (N.S.W.); A. & P. Act 1969 Pt. III (N.T.); Succession Act 1981 Pt. III (Qld.); A. & P. Act 1919 Pt. IIIA (S.A.); A. & P. Act 1935 Pt. V (Tas.); A. & P. Act 1958 Pt I (Vic.); Administration Act 1903 Pt. II (W.A.).
22   Family Provision Act (F. P.) 1969 (A.C.T.); F. P. Act 1982 (N.S.W.); F. P. Act 1979 (N.T.); Succession Act 1981 (Qld.); Inheritance (F. P. Act 1972 (S.A.); A. & P. Act 1958 (Vic.); Testators Family Maintenance Act 1957 (Tas.); Inheritance (Family and Dependant's Provision) Act 1972 (W.A.).

relationships. Indeed, historically, even the relationship of marriage was discounted on inheritance – spouses were not regarded as heirs-at-law and were insignificant as next-of-kin, and it took modern statutory treatment of inheritance to put spouses into the dominant position in intestacy law.[23] Blood was so important that a distinction was made between whole-blood and half-blood relatives. Traditionally these could only be whole-blood relatives in relation to land, although this distinction was not made in relation to personal property.[24] This distinction still operates in the New South Wales intestacy legislation,[25] although most Australian states have abolished it.

The twentieth century saw an increasing emphasis in the legislation on the role of the spouse – in intestacy and family provision jurisdictions the spouse may be the sole inheritor, depending on the size of the estate. Indeed the spouse is now seen as so important that the definition of spouse for the purposes of intestacy and family provision may include the legal spouse, the *de facto* spouse and even former spouses. This may reflect the latter twentieth century emphasis on the nuclear family.[26]

The following table (Kinship Diagram 1) is a picture of how I (a non-Aboriginal descendant of British people who came to Australia in the 1850s) would speak of my relatives. The fact that I am female does not change what I call various people – my brother would use the same terms and expect the same sorts of behaviour from these people. For example, I would as a child have seen my mother as very different from my aunts – my mother was primary caregiver and I rarely saw my aunts. The position was the same for my brother. The characteristics of my kinship pattern include the emphasis on blood to define relationships, and the lineal tracing of relationships being emphasised more than the collateral.

Diane Bell explains what an Aranda person would say of the same relationships.[27] In Kinship Diagram 2 the propositus here is also female:

---

[23]   The heir-at-law for the common law in relation to land was generally the eldest son. In France this was all the sons who could inherit land during middle ages, early modern and modern times.

[24]   *Watts v Crooke* (1690) Show. 108; 1 E. R. 74 (H. L.).

[25]   N.S.W. Wills Probate and Administration Act 1898, s. 61 B(6).

[26]   See, for example, Peter McDonald, *Family Trends and Structure in Australia*, Australian Family Briefings No 3, Australian Institute of Family Studies (1993), and Part One: The Social and Conceptual Context in J. Eekelaar and M. Maclean (eds) *A Reader on Family Law*, Oxford Readings in Socio-legal Studies (1994). In the Succession Context see Chapter 3, *The Relationships of Succession: the Family* in Atherton and Vines, *Australian Succession Law; Families, Property and Death*, Butterworths, Sydney (1996).

[27]   Diane Bell, *Daughters of the Dreaming*, McPhee Gribble Publishers, Melbourne (1983), Appendix 2.

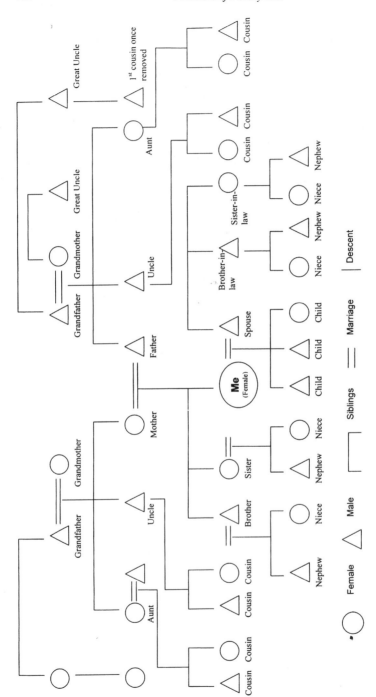

Kinship Diagram 1

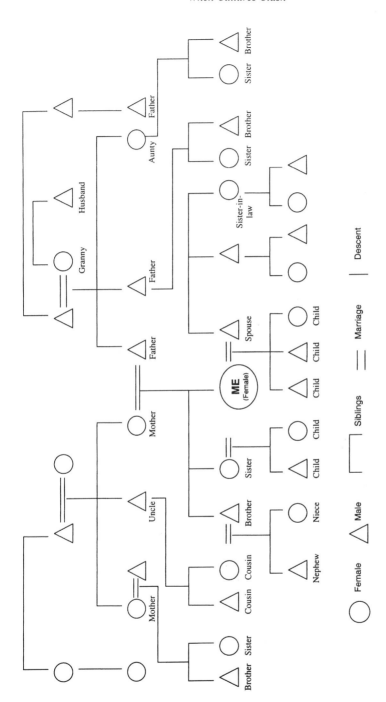

Kinship Diagram 2

Aboriginal definitions of family

The second diagram shows an Aranda kinship system. Not all Aboriginal kinship patterns are the same, of course, but they tend to share the kind of emphases shown here. As Bell explains it, terms which are used lineally for my relationship grid are used collaterally for the Aranda system. A male's kinship terms would be different again. She also notes that for Aranda, in one's own generation is included all siblings, one's grandparents and their siblings, one's grandchildren; in the other generation are one's parents and siblings, one's children and all their cousins. This way of thinking about generations is one which treats kinship as a sort of circle rather than as a long lineal trail.

There are further complications in that groups are also divided into moieties which may determine who may marry whom etc. Radcliffe-Brown explained the kinship systems according to these principles, stated by Ian Keen:

> Aboriginal society gives the widest possible recognition to genealogical relationships. Systems of kin classification are governed by three principles: the equivalence of brothers; the bringing of relatives by marriage within the classes of consanguineal relatives; and, although every term has a primary meaning, the non-limitation of range. There is a certain pattern of behaviour for each kind of relative, and the kinship system regulates marriage.[28]

One thing he does not mention here is the importance of adoption and the willingness to recognise kinship without benefit of a blood relationship.

Although there are differences amongst kinship groups, and these patterns may be looser or tighter, the description remains valid to explain the poor fit between the family structure contemplated by the statutory intestacy regimes for non-Aboriginal people and the kinship structures which Aborigines recognise.

The striking thing for us, looking at Bell's table, is to see how many people would be regarded as *father*, for example, and how differently the children of one's same-sex sibling are regarded compared with the children of one's opposite-sex sibling. Only terminology is shown here, but the terminology reflects customary law obligations and dependencies which are woven into the social fabric. The kinship structure is a structure of obligations and dependency. The number of children that an Aboriginal woman would have depending on her for nurture may include children we would refer to as her children, grandchildren, nieces, nephews and further beyond. In the context of non-Aboriginal succession law those obligations would give rise to the very moral obligations one would expect the testator to give weight to in making a will, or in Family Provision law,[29] although the kinship group would not extend so far.

---

[28]   I. Keen, *Kinship*, in R. M. Berndt and R. Tonkinson, (eds.) *Social Anthropology and Australian Aboriginal Studies*, Aboriginal Studies Press, Canberra, (1988) at p. 80. See also Peter Sutton, *Native Title and the Descent of Rights*, National Native Title Tribunal, Perth, (1998).

[29]   Sometimes known as Testator's Family Maintenance legislation.

Statutory inheritance regimes for Aboriginal and Torres Strait Islander people

General issues

Only Queensland, Western Australia and the Northern Territory have specific regimes available to Aboriginal people. However, examination of the legislation shows that only the Northern Territory has really tried to grapple with the concept that customary law may have different ideas about inheritance than our normal inheritance regimes offer. In relation to intestacy, the Queensland Law Reform Commission decided that this was too hard:[30]

> Knowledge of Aboriginal and Torres Strait Islander customary law is incomplete and fragmented. It would therefore be insufficient for the Commission to make any confident recommendation concerning its integration with existing succession law... . Until extensive work has been done to bring knowledge of customary law clearly into focus and widespread consultation has been initiated and brought to fruition, the Commission is of the view that it could be counter-productive, even misleading, to introduce legislation at the present time purporting to affect customary law, or to recognise it, in the narrow context of intestacy rules.

Some historical patterns may be discerned in the legislation. In these three jurisdictions legislation on intestacy has arisen in a number of stages. First, early case law[31] and the legislation took no note of traditional customary law marriage. This created two problems – it automatically put Aboriginal spouses (often multiple, since polygyny was widely practiced) into the *de facto* class at a time when *de facto* spouses had no rights, and it made the children of such unions illegitimate at a time when an illegitimate child also had no rights of inheritance.

This position was rectified in the 1970s when there was recognition that at least some kind of recognition of customary law was required. However, this tended to be limited to recognition of traditional marriage. This did not solve the problem, but in turn created difficulties, because of the tendency to use traditional marriage to define a person as a traditional person. However, it did make the standard intestacy legislation slightly more meaningful to Aboriginal people.

In the nineteen-eighties and nineties, *de facto* spouses in all Australian jurisdictions were placed in a position equivalent or very similar to that of legal spouses for many purposes including inheritance.[32] Children's status, similarly, is

---

30   Qld Law Reform Commission *Report No. 42 Intestacy Rules*, (1993), pp.12-13.

31   For example, *R v Neddy Monkey* [1861] V.L.R. (L.) 40 at p.41 the court decided not to take judicial notice of 'vague rites and ceremonies' in relation to an issue of the marital status of the defendant and the chief prosecution witness. Similarly in *R v Cobby* (1883) 4 N.S.W.L.R. 355 at p.356 the court did not recognise an Aboriginal marriage because the aborigines 'have no laws of which we can have cognizance'.

32   W.P.A. Act (N.S.W.) s.32G (intestacy) Family Provision Act 1982 s.6; A.& P. Act 1969 (N.T.) s.6(1); Succession Act (Qld.) s.40 (family provision); A. & P. Act 1919 (S.A.) Pt.IIIA (intestacy); Inheritance (Family Provision) Act (S.A.) s.4

no longer regulated by whether their parents are legally married.[33] This prevented the stigma of illegitimacy for children and ensured parent-child inheritance could operate, but it did not help with whether a person was a traditional Aboriginal or not.

Current regimes specifically for Aboriginal people

Queensland, Western Australia and the Northern Territory are the only jurisdictions which have attempted to set up inheritance regimes specifically for Aboriginal people. These three jurisdictions are those with the highest indigenous populations. However, the way the regimes have been set up indicates the power of some of the myths considered earlier. One of the most powerful is the myth that Aborigines are either traditional or not traditional. All the regimes can be overridden by a will made by the deceased. If there is no will (and Aborigines have a very low rate of testacy in Australia) then there is a threshold test to determine whether the specific legislation applies. This test takes the form of determining identity as Aboriginal either by blood or by the existence of a traditional marriage. Only the Northern Territory has really grappled with attempting to recognise customary law of succession (rather than just customary law of marriage) in its legislation.

Queensland   In Queensland the Community Services (Aborigines) Act 1984 and its counterpart the Community Services (Torres Strait Islanders) Act 1984 refer specifically to intestate Aboriginal and Torres Strait Islander succession. Section 75 of the Community Services (Aborigines) Act[34] gives the power to decide who is entitled to succeed to the estate of an intestate Aborigine to the Chief Executive. If no-one can be found to succeed, the estate vests in the chief executive who is to use the money for the benefit of Aborigines generally as provided by s.71 (Grant of Aid). The Chief Executive is defined by s.7 as 'the officer charged with the responsibility for the administration of this Act, subject to the Minister'. This is the Under Secretary of the Department. A startling section is section 75(2):

> (2) A certificate purporting to be signed by the chief executive that the person or persons named therein is or are entitled to succeed to the estate or any part of the estate of the person named therein … or that there is no person so entitled shall be conclusive evidence of the matters contained therein.

(family provision); Inheritance (Family and Dependants Provision) Amendment Act 1986 (W.A.) s.7 (family provision).

[33] Birth (Equality of Status) Act 1988 (A.C.T.); Wills Act 1968 (A.C.T.) s. 31A; Status of Children Act 1996 (N.S.W.); Status of Children Act 1978 (NT); Status of Children Act 1978 (Qld); Family Relationships Act 1975 (SA); Status of Children Act 1974 (Tas); Status of Children Act 1974 (Vic); Wills Act 1970 (WA) s.31(wills); Inheritance (Family and Dependants) Provision Act 1972; Administration Act 1903 (WA) s. 12A (intestacy).

[34] Corresponds to s. 73 Community Services (Torres Strait Islanders) Act 1984.

This part of the Act almost exactly mirrors the previous legislation, the Aborigines Act 1971 (Qld), which was criticised as giving 'a highly arbitrary power by which persons who would otherwise be entitled to succeed on intestacy may be excluded solely on the basis of the Director's [replaced by Chief Executive in 1984 legislation] determination that it is "impractical" to ascertain who they are ...'. This criticism goes on to note that '... It comes close to an arbitrary deprivation of property within Article 17(2) of the Universal Declaration of Human Rights'.[35] The criticism was clearly not taken to heart when the 1984 Act was passed.

When is a person an Aboriginal to whom this Act applies? It is not defined in the Act, but the definition used generally in Queensland is 'a person who is a member of the Aboriginal race of Australia'. The Community Services Acts clearly operate to diminish rather than expand the autonomy of the people it purports to assist and does so by a mechanism which gives a massive level of discretion to the Under Secretary of the Department.

Western Australia   In Western Australia, there is a special section dealing with customary law for intestacy. Section 35 of the Aboriginal Affairs Planning Authority Act 1972 provides, *inter alia*:

> 35(1) All property and rights of property vested in any person of Aboriginal descent who dies intestate shall vest in the Public Trustee under and subject to the provisions of the Public Trustee Act 1941 upon trust to pay the just debts of the deceased and to distribute the balance amongst the persons entitled thereto according to the laws of the State relating to the administration of estates of persons dying intestate, if any of the persons so entitled can be ascertained, otherwise amongst those persons who may by regulation be prescribed as the persons entitled to succeed to the property of the deceased.
>
> (2) A regulation made for the purposes of this section shall, so far as that is practicable, provide for the distribution of the estate in accordance with the Aboriginal customary law as it applied to the deceased at the time of his death.

This provision only applies if the deceased has not made a will. If no person can be found to take under s. 35 then the Public Trustee is required to hold the estate for the benefit of 'persons of Aboriginal descent'.

'Persons of Aboriginal Descent' are defined in the Act as:

> any person living in Western Australia wholly or partly descended from the original inhabitants of Australia who claims to be an Aboriginal and who is accepted as such in the community in which he lives.

This is a blood-line definition, and s.33 provides that:

---

[35]   G. Nettheim, *Victims of the Law: Black Queenslanders today*, Allen and Unwin, (1981) at p.90.

> The provisions of this Part apply to and in relation to a person of Aboriginal descent only if he is also of the full blood descended from the original inhabitants of Australia or more than one-fourth of the full blood.

Thus, if a person who is less than one-fourth Aboriginal blood dies intestate, who inherits their estate will be determined by the Administration and Probate Act (W.A.) rather than the Aboriginal Affairs Planning Authority Act. This is the case even if the person has been living within and identifying with the Aboriginal community.

If a person dies who is more than one-fourth of the full blood, then their estate vests in the Public Trustee. When the Aboriginal Affairs Planning Authority Act was introduced into Parliament, part of the Second Reading Speech[36] said:

> Briefly, if the Public Trustee is unable to ascertain who is entitled to benefit under the normal laws of the State, any balance remaining may be distributed in accordance with the Aboriginal customary law as it applied to the deceased at the time of his death.

However, reg. 9(1)(b) stipulates that if a person has been married 'in accordance with the laws relating to marriage' (that is, the Marriage Act 1961 (Cth)) their estate is not to be dealt with by the Public Trustee according to this section.

This aspect of the Act and Regulations partakes of the myth that a person is either traditional Aboriginal or not. It assumes that if a person has been formally married under the Marriage Act that they are not living any aspect of a traditional lifestyle. This assumption is not justified. To begin with, one of the few non-traditional things an Aboriginal person living a traditional life on a reserve with a mission might have done was to have been married according to the Marriage Act, because of the presence of missionaries. Similarly, many Aboriginal people lived fairly traditional lives incorporated with being stockmen on stations and so on. They also were quite likely to have been married under the Marriage Act. This was noted by the Australian Law Reform Commission Report as well.[37]

There is some question about the validity of the regulations (especially reg. 9(2) 'notwithstanding any tribal law or custom to the contrary') given the references to customary law in both s.35 and the Second Reading Speech. Are they *ultra vires*? The regulations clearly give no recognition to customary law at all. The Aboriginal Legal Service of Western Australia (A.L.S.W.A.) has submitted to the W.A.L.R.C. that the regulations may be *ultra vires* on this basis.

The Act proceeds in steps and regulation 9 spells the steps out – if one is regarded as Aboriginal then the ordinary rules will apply unless the Public Trustee cannot find the proper recipients; the next step is a distribution which at first glance appears to take some cognizance of customary law. The Act does not say how that is to be determined, requiring only the satisfaction of the Public Trustee. Regulation 9 spells out which traditional or customary law persons will benefit. The extent of customary law which is recognised under this law is absolutely

---

36   W.A. House of Assembly, Hansard, Thursday 11 May 1972.
37   A.L.R.C. *The Recognition of Aboriginal Customary Law*, (1986) Vol. 1, p.230.

minimal. It only goes so far as to recognise traditional marriage and the children of that marriage as legitimate. There is no attempt to reflect customary law obligations or inheritance that would traditionally follow from those relationships. Regulation 9 specifies that the persons entitled to the estate are:

1. Where the deceased was male his customary law ('according to the social structure of the tribe to which he belonged') wife if they had a child or children and those children, in equal shares *per capita*.
2. Where the deceased was female, her husband, whether or not they had children.
3. The children of traditional marriage in equal shares.
4. If none of the above survive, the deceased's father 'by reason of a tribal marriage'.
5. If none of the above survive, the deceased's mother 'by reason of a tribal marriage'.
6. If none of the above survive, then in trust for the benefit of Aboriginal people in general.

Where no-one appears entitled to succeed, the Public Trustee holds the estate for the benefit of Aboriginals generally. The Public Trustee is entitled to a fee for this service, which is a proportion of the estate.

Section 35(2) suggests that customary law will apply to the regulations, but the list above shows how minimal that customary law recognition is. The kinship structure implied by the list above is even more linear and shorter than the one used for non-Aboriginal people. There is no room for collateral relatives. The list of relatives who take on intestacy is shorter than the list in the Administration and Probate Act. In the absence of spouse or issue of the deceased, the Administration and Probate Act allows the estate to pass to parents, grandparents and uncles and aunts and their children before it reverts to the Crown. This is the case 'notwithstanding any tribal law or custom to the contrary' (reg. 9(2)). This is an extraordinary truncation of the obligations of relationships, made even more extraordinary by the knowledge of the extent and meaning of kinship ties in Aboriginal communities reflected in the diagrams above. The meaning of 'by reason of a tribal marriage' in reg. 9 is unclear. Perhaps it reflects the knowledge that the term 'father' might apply in traditional law to many people, as in the kinship diagrams above. However it might also reflect a complete lack of knowledge and merely be attempting to treat traditional marriage as the legitimator of children. One suspects that the latter is true.

The only variation recognised is s.35(3) and reg. 9(5) which allow a person with a moral claim to apply for assistance. This moral claim is likely to be the kind of moral claim used in family provision matters.

The real thrust of this legislation is paternalistic rather than the expedition of customary law in any way. What the legislation does is remove the estate, which is likely to be small given the demographic profile of Aboriginal people, from the control of the next of kin (who is likely to be Aboriginal), and give it to the Public

Trustee at a fee which will diminish the size of the estate. This in itself appears to be discriminatory, as A.L.S.W.A. has argued.

A.L.S.W.A. has also argued that the definition of Aboriginal in s.33 is contrary to s.10 of the Racial Discrimination Act (Cth.).[38] Their submission observes at page 2:

> It should be noted that neither the exclusive categories provided for in the *Administration Act* or the *Inheritance (Family and Dependants Provision) Act* are necessarily appropriate to Aboriginal persons particularly in view of Aboriginal kinship systems and classificatory relatives.

They further note that time limits impact especially severely on Aboriginal people. Six month time limits for initiating legal process are not sensible when people may be out in the desert for months, and this is especially true in a jurisdiction like Western Australia which has a territory of over one million square miles/2.5 million square kilometres.

Northern Territory   In the Northern Territory the Status of Children Act 1978 (N.T.) s.3 defines an Aboriginal marriage as 'a relationship between a man and woman that is recognized as a traditional marriage by the community or group to which they belong'. The Northern Territory's Family Provision legislation has a similar definition[39] and continues 'and all relationships shall be determined accordingly'. This brings traditional marriage within the standard intestacy and family provision legislation.

The Northern Territory has made a concerted effort to recognise customary law in the area of intestacy. In 1979 the Territory inserted into the Administration and Probate Act, Division 4A, Intestate Aboriginals. This used the same definition for Aboriginal marriage as the Family Provision and Status of Children legislation. Division 4A was intended to apply to Aboriginals living a traditional lifestyle. In Parliament, the Chief Minister, when presenting the bill, said:[40]

> The purpose of this act is to enable, in the case of intestate Aboriginals, people who would be able to share in the estate of a deceased Aboriginal in accordance with tribal custom to approach the court and get an order for distribution of the estate in accordance with tribal custom.

The Act contemplates by s.71B that where an Aboriginal has died intestate, a person who claims entitlement under the customs or traditions (or the Public Trustee) may apply for an order for distribution. The application is supposed to be

---

[38]   Aboriginal Legal Service of W.A. *Submission to the Western Australian Government on Changes Needed to the Laws dealing with Intestate Estates of Aboriginal Persons*, 15 September, 1995, manuscript in possession of the author.

[39]   Section 7 (1A) of the N.T. Family Provision Act 1980 provides that 'an Aboriginal who has entered into a relationship with another Aboriginal that is recognised as traditional marriage by the community or group to which either Aboriginal belongs is married to the other Aboriginal ...'

[40]   N.T. Parliamentary Debates, Thursday, 23 November, 1978.

accompanied by a 'plan of distribution of the intestate estate prepared in accordance with the traditions of the community or group to which the intestate Aboriginal belonged'. There is an initial time limit of 6 months, but that can be extended if the court thinks it is necessary.

The Court, when making its order, must take into account the plan prepared and the traditions of the community or group; further, the Court is not to make an order for distribution unless it is satisfied of its justice in all the circumstances. This section, s.71E, imports a large level of discretion into the court's deliberations. The provisions are also subject to any Family Provision order which has been made.

This is a real attempt to deal with the fact that Aboriginal customary law cannot be dealt with as a monolith. Thus the legislation has grappled with one of the myths discussed above. However, it has not grappled with another, because, by s.71 the whole Division 4A only applies if an intestate Aboriginal has not entered into a marriage that is a valid marriage under the *Marriage Act 1961 (Cth.)*.

Options for recognising customary law in inheritance

Difficulties

A number of options have been considered for allowing customary law to operate in Australia. There is currently some recognition of customary law for the purposes of sentencing,[41] for the purpose of native title[42] land and at times for the purpose of assessing damages in civil law cases.[43] Customary law regulation of personal relationships is to some extent recognised, but outside particular areas or districts where community customary law may operate, and except for the above instances, customary law is not influential. There are great difficulties with it. Firstly, often customary law is secret and informing a whitefella court of it will damage it by making it public. This is an issue that has been constantly confronted in the context of land claims. Secondly from the common law side, having satisfactory evidence of the customary law is extremely difficult. Using A.T.S.I.C.[44] and Land Councils will not be satisfactory because those groups as representative bodies will not necessarily have the expertise which is needed to deal with a particular dispute, and they may indeed not come from the proper area. In the context of inheritance in particular there is another issue which is what should be done when an Aboriginal

---

41   In sentencing courts should at least consider the customary law which would apply to the offence: *R v Minor* (1992) 79 N.T.R. 1 (C.C.A.). Sometimes customary law sanctions may lead to a lesser 'whitefella' sentence : eg *R v Jungarai*, unrep, N.T. Sup. Ct., Muirhead J., 2 Nov 1981. But note that sometimes whitefella law is the only barrier between Aboriginal women and domestic violence. See McRae, Nettheim and Beacroft, *Indigenous Legal Issues*, 2nd ed., L.B.C., Sydney, (1997).

42   *Mabo v Qld* (No. 2) (1992) 175 C.L.R. 1.

43   E.g. *Napaluma v Baker* Unreported N.T.; cited in *Dixon v Davies* (1982) 17 N.T.R. 31. Napaluma's damages for head injuries were increased in recognition that under customary law he could no longer be initiated fully as a man into his tribe.

44   The Aboriginal and Torres Strait Islanders Commission.

person has married a non-Aboriginal person. This paper does not attempt to resolve this issue. Many other difficulties remain. What is needed is a system which can identify customary law and take account of the variety of customary law, can deal with conflict about what the customary law is, and can accommodate the varieties of indigenous life experience within traditional, kinship and other obligations (including the relationship with non-indigenous society).

Assessors

One solution has been tried in South Australia for dispute resolution under the Pitjatjantjara Land Rights Act 1981 (S.A.). Under this Act the Minister with the approval of the Aboriginal council from the area can appoint a tribal assessor who is required to 'give effect to the customs and traditions of the Pitjatjantjara people' (s.36(4)). A similar provision exists in the Maralinga Tjarutja Land Rights Act 1983 (S.A.). This way of dealing with customary law apparently derives from African models.[45] The assessor approach is attractive at first sight – but clearly there need to be multiple assessors. Where the customary law of small groups is at issue, only assessors within that group would be knowledgeable enough, but they are likely to have a personal stake in the outcome. There is apparently some concern in Africa with the use of these models because they do not manage disputes over the meaning of customary law very well.[46]

The Northern Territory model

The Northern Territory's model for dealing with customary law in inheritance is the best of the models on offer, particularly if the requirement not to have been in a Marriage Act marriage is removed. However, there remain issues about how to determine what the customary law is, and how to deal with disputes about it. What if the women and the men think differently about what the customary law is? What if the customary law appears to breach human rights ideas which the Australian common law holds dear? The common law generally rejects law which offends the latter ideas. However, the evidentiary problem is a real one. Where there are multiple customary laws how do we decide between them?

Changing intestacy legislation

All these issues need to be considered – but they are often a last resort. The first step should be to extend the kinship group who are regarded as entitled on intestacy to consideration. This should be done for Aboriginal people[47] but not for non-Aboriginal people, and it should be done in all the Australian jurisdictions.

---

45   P. Hennessy, *Aboriginal Customary Law and Local Justice Mechanisms: Principles, Options and Proposals* A.L.R.C. Research Paper, (1984).

46   Conversation of the author with Abdul Paliwala, Warwick University, United Kingdom, May 2001.

47   For this purpose a definition of Aboriginal which includes identification with and by the group should be used.

The regime should apply to Aboriginal people on the basis of the normal test for Aboriginality – do they identify as Aboriginal and does the Aboriginal community recognise them as Aboriginal? The Northern Territory model seems a good one to work from. There are a number of reasons for Aboriginal intestacy. One of them is simply poverty. Poor people are less likely to make wills than wealthy people, probably for two reasons – first, they feel they have less to leave, and secondly, they do not have access to a solicitor who could draft it for them. The major time most Australians make wills is when they have just bought a house – and the solicitor does a will for them. Aboriginal people have a vastly lower home ownership rate than non-indigenous people. The importance of intestacy legislation is that it operates automatically – it gives rights to people, not mere expectations. All one has to do is show that one is in the relevant group and the right arises – it does not need a court to determine it in most circumstances. This is an advantage over family provision legislation. However, intestacy legislation at present deals with the estate as a whole and makes no distinction between land and chattels or significant objects, so it tends to be a blunt instrument.

Changing Family Provision legislation

Similar changes and on the same basis could be made to Family Provision legislation. This raises a policy issue about wills and the extent to which the testator's wishes can be circumvented. Of course, the problem with wills is that tough-minded testators sometimes leave all their property away from the people who seem most entitled to it. The Family Provision legislation applies in this situation. At present Family Provision legislation does not match the kinship patterns of Aboriginal and Torres Strait Islander people. Recognition of those kinship patterns within the Family Provision legislation of all Australian jurisdictions would have the great advantage of then allowing a discretionary consideration of all possible applicants – including those under customary law and those considered needy under the ordinary law.

However, making changes to Family Provision legislation without making changes to intestacy regimes would not be a good idea. A family provision claim requires a court hearing, with associated costs and difficulty – thus family provision gives expectations and not rights and will solve few problems. However, one advantage of family provision jurisdiction is that the court is able to remake the will and thus distinguish between various kinds of property and various kinds of needs – thus there can be some delicacy in the way the estate is dealt with using this jurisdiction.

Wills as shields and spears

Recognising customary law in inheritance is obviously important. The first step should be to extend the kinship group entitled on inheritance to one matching customary law patterns. The Northern Territory model is the best one on offer, (if the requirement not to have been in a Marriage Act marriage is removed) because it allows for the recognition of different patterns of customary law amongst different groups. Similarly, eligible applicants for family provision should be extended where the deceased is Aboriginal.

Intestacy legislation is important in this context because it operates automatically. Thus it offers a right rather than a mere expectation which has to be argued for in court. This is its advantage. Its disadvantage is that it may not be precise enough to deal with specific types of property and with both custodial and commodity property.

Intestacy regimes deal with the estate as a whole, whereas wills and customary law have the capacity to deal separately with different types of property and therefore also with differences between obligations, rights, and what one might call custodial and 'commodified' property. That is one reason to use wills to allow customary law obligations to be given the force of common law.

It is crucial to increase the number of Aborigines who make wills, and to ensure that when they make wills they have will drafters who understand the problems of terminology for kinship terms (such as 'father', as we have seen above) and can draft accordingly. Drafting wills to protect customary law obligations and general property rights for Aboriginal people might call for a considered use of testamentary trusts including secret and half-secret trusts, discretionary trusts, and life estates. For example, wills can ensure that customary law obligations spelt out in the will (or even as half-secret trusts to ensure confidentiality) will be recognised and given legal force by the common law. Wills can deal precisely with a range of property and obligations. They can deal with commodity property by giving it away or organising for it to be held in trust for persons to whom there are obligations. They can deal with custodianship as well, by creating trust relationships, and, for example, by the use of secret or half-secret trusts, set up a situation where a person is entitled to keep cultural information such as traditional medicine secrets and pass it on. Guardianship and control of children may also be important. All these constructs are ways of protecting information or people, and they may be far easier to protect if they are established by will than by *inter vivos* gift in a customary law context. Wills may also, once admitted to probate, be able to operate as evidentiary material for future claims.

Discussions with Aboriginal Legal Service lawyers have been met with the statement that they have more than enough to deal with at present – their legal aid budget does not include will-making, and is more than stretched when dealing with criminal law, domestic violence, tenancy and so on. In my view only dedicated grants would deal properly with this. In the present political climate it seems highly unlikely that a budget dedicated to Aboriginal will-making would be established, but in the meantime, recognition by lawyers generally that *pro bono* work might be directed this way would be a help. At present the barriers to will-making for Aboriginal people seem immense, but they are not insurmountable. Work on developing suitable precedents and reducing expense is needed.

Conclusion

This chapter has shown how unsatisfactory is the present regime of recognition of the inheritance needs of Aboriginal people in Australia. The regime fails to recognise the impact of the different cultures in very many ways, not least being the failure to recognise the different kinship patterns of Aboriginals and Torres Strait Islanders and their impact in inheritance law and the failure to recognise the importance of custodial property for intestacy (with the possible exception of the Northern Territory). The recognition of Aboriginal customary law in respect of inheritance is an extremely complex issue. No simple solution is likely to be satisfactory, and satisfactory solutions are unlikely to be cheap. The danger of destroying customary law by breaching secrecy is a real danger which needs to be constructively addressed. Until we have more satisfactory systems, the structure of the inheritance systems in all the Australian jurisdictions means that making wills which recognise Aboriginal customary law may be the best way to proceed to ensure both the protection and enforcement of customary law in relation to inheritance.

Chapter 8

Pre-nuptial Agreements and Financial Provision

Gareth Miller

Introduction

Formal agreements between prospective spouses made in contemplation of marriage to govern their proprietary and financial rights *inter se* during marriage and, more particularly, on the termination of marriage by death or divorce, have traditionally been regarded as unenforceable in English law.[1] This was re-affirmed by Wall J. in the recent case of *N v. N (Jurisdiction: Pre-nuptial Agreement)*.[2] The hostility to pre-nuptial agreements traditionally found in English law, and reflected in other common law jurisdictions, is in contrast to the recognition of such agreements in other legal systems where such agreements are often an integral part of the arrangements made on marriage. English courts have long had to consider the effect of such agreements which have been validly made under another legal system when a marriage has been terminated by the death of a spouse. They are increasingly having to consider the effect of such agreements made before the parties to the marriage acquired any connection with England and Wales in proceedings following the breakdown of the marriage. Such agreements are now possible under legislation in a number of common law jurisdictions,[3] and there is increasing pressure for English law to 'recognise' the validity of pre-nuptial agreements made in England. Indeed, in recent cases the courts have had to consider the effect of pre-nuptial agreements made in England.[4] Even if they are 'unenforceable', that does not mean that they are necessarily without effect. In

---

1   The term 'pre-nuptial agreement' will be used in preference to the term 'ante-nuptial agreement'.

2   [1999] 2 F.L.R. 745 at p.751.

3   See the Matrimonial Property Act 1976 in New Zealand; Part VIIIA of the Family Law Act 1975 (inserted by the Family Law Amendment Act 2000) in Australia and in the United States the Uniform Premarital Agreement Act which, or parts of which, have been adopted in some twenty states. See further Nasheri, *Premarital Agreements in the United States: A Need for Closer Control?* (1998) 12 I.J.L.P.F. 307 and Fehlberg and Smyth, *Binding Pre-Nuptial Agreements in Australia: The First Year* (2002) 16 I.J.L.P.F.127.

4   See *K v. K (Ancillary Relief: Prenuptial Agreement)* [2003] 1 F.L.R. 120; *G v. G (Financial Provision: Separation Agreement)* [2000] 2 F.L.R. 18; *Wyatt-Jones v. Goldsmith* (2000) WL 976036.

their Consultation Document, *Supporting Families*,[5] the Government expresses a desire to do what it can to strengthen marriage and among the proposals is one to:

> Make pre-nuptial written agreements about the distribution of money and property legally binding, for those who wish to use them.[6]

What are the merits of such a proposal and what are the dangers? Although these questions can, and must be addressed at a general level, it is also essential to consider them in relation to the ways in which pre-nuptial agreements may be 'recognised'. What is meant by making such agreements 'legally binding'? In what way would this differ from the treatment of pre-nuptial agreements by the English courts at the present time? What are the merits of 'legally binding' pre-nuptial agreements?

Arrangements which are recognised

Ante-nuptial settlements

Ante-nuptial settlements of property for the benefit of the parties to a marriage and their children have long received recognition from English law as have post-nuptial settlements. In *N v. N* Wall J. said:[7]

> The difference between an antenuptial settlement and an antenuptial contract or agreement is that the former seeks to regulate the financial affairs of the spouses on and during their marriage. It does not contemplate the dissolution of the marriage. By contrast, an agreement made prior to marriage which contemplates the steps the parties will take in the event of divorce or separation is perceived as being contrary to public policy because it undermines the concept of marriage as a life-long union.

It must be remembered that such settlements have been, and remain, subject to variation court on termination of a marriage by divorce or on the death of a spouse.[8]

Agreements on the breakdown of marriage

English law has for some time permitted agreements relating to financial provision between spouses who have already separated.[9] Indeed, following the Divorce

---

5   Home Office (1998).

6   Ibid., para.4.12.

7   [1999] 2 F.L.R. 745 at p.752.

8   Matrimonial Causes Act 1973, s.24(1)(c) and (d); Inheritance (Provision for Family and Dependants) Act 1975, s.2(1)(f).

9   In *Fender v. St.John Mildmay* [1938] A.C. 1 at p 44, Lord Wright said that while an agreement for future separation was against the policy of the law, if 'a

Reform Act 1969 it has been the policy to encourage parties to a marriage to reach agreement regarding property and financial matters. However, while such agreements are encouraged they cannot oust the jurisdiction of the court and, while they may be accorded great weight, the court may in appropriate cases vary their effect by making orders for financial provision and property adjustment. The principles to be applied in considering the effect of such agreements were set out by the Court of Appeal in *Edgar v. Edgar*[10] in 1980. The Inheritance (Provision for Family and Dependants) Act 1975 expressly provided a means whereby, during the lifetime of a spouse, the right of the other spouse to apply for provision out of his or her estate can be barred by agreement between the spouses. However, such an agreement is only effective if incorporated in an order of the court in proceedings for divorce, nullity or judicial separation.[11]

Pre-nuptial agreements made abroad

Pre-nuptial agreements made in other jurisdictions have been accorded recognition by English courts on the death of a party. Thus in *De Nichols v. Curlier*[12] the House of Lords held that the rights created by an implied agreement under French law were not affected by the fact that the parties had subsequently become domiciled in England. This meant that the wife was entitled to one half of the substantial movable property acquired in the husband's name so that on his death he could dispose of only one half of that property. However, while such agreements may be recognised as establishing existing property rights of the spouses, there seems little doubt that the proprietary rights determined by such an agreement would be subject to the powers of the court under the Inheritance (Provision for Family and Dependants) Act 1975 to order provision out of the estate of the deceased spouse provided he was domiciled in England at the time of his death. There is no English decision in point, but in relation to similar legislation the High Court of Australia in *Singer v. Berghouse*[13] held that an ante-nuptial agreement was admissible for the limited purpose of showing that the parties thought its terms fair at the time they signed it.

In the context of divorce the courts have had to consider the effect of pre-nuptial agreements in three situations: (i) when a court is exercising its powers to order financial provision and property adjustment on divorce under the Matrimonial Causes Act 1973; (ii) when the court is determining whether to grant a stay of divorce proceedings in England where divorce proceedings are also pending in another jurisdiction; (iii) when the court is determining whether or not leave should

---

separation has actually occurred or becomes inevitable, the law allows the matter to be dealt with according to realities and not according to a fiction.'

10   [1980] 1 W.L.R. 1418.
11   s.15.
12   [1900] A.C. 21. See also *Re De Nicholls* [1900] 2 Ch. 21; *Chiwell v. Carylon* (1897) 14 S C 61 and dicta of Richardson J. in *Walker v. Walker* [1983] N.Z.L.R. 560 at p.574.
13   (1994) 181 C.L.R. 201 at pp.207-208.

be granted under the Matrimonial Proceedings and Property Act 1984 to enable financial provision to be sought following a divorce in another jurisdiction.

The exercise of the powers under the Matrimonial Causes Act 1973 When a court is exercising the powers to order financial provision and property adjustment under the Matrimonial Causes Act 1973 it is not bound by the terms of a pre-nuptial contract determining the allocation of resources on divorce even though the contract is valid in the country in which it was made. Moreover, such contracts may carry little weight with the court in the exercise of its discretion. Thus in *F v. F (Ancillary Relief: Substantial Assets)*[14] Thorpe J. said:

> The rights and responsibilities of those whose financial affairs are regulated by statute cannot be much influenced by contractual terms which were *devised for the control and limitation of standards that are intended to be of universal application throughout our society.*

However, although a pre-nuptial contract is not binding on a court, there may be cases in which it could prove to be a significant factor. In *S v. S (Divorce: Staying Proceedings)* Wilson J. said:[15]

> I am aware of a growing belief that, in the despatch of a claim for ancillary relief in this jurisdiction, no significant weight will be afforded to a prenuptial agreement, whatever the circumstances. I would like to sound a cautionary note in that respect.

Expressing profound respect for the observations of Thorpe L.J. in *F v. F (Ancillary Relief: Substantial Assets)* quoted above, he went on to say:[16]

> There is a danger that these wide words might be taken out of context. There is no doubt that, where the English court proceeds to determine an application for ancillary relief, s.25 of the 1973 Act precludes any choice of foreign law, however vividly the circumstances of the case might protest its relevance. So the application is of English law and under s.25(1) regard must be had to all the circumstances of the case. In *F v. F* itself, the result of a strict application of the effect of the prenuptial agreements would have been, as the judge said, 'ridiculous'. In those circumstances they inevitably constituted circumstances of negligible significance. But there will come a case – were I to refuse a stay, might this be it? – where the circumstances surrounding the prenuptial agreement and the provision therein contained might, when viewed in the context of the other circumstances of the case, prove influential or even crucial. *Where other jurisdictions, both in the USA and in the European Union, have been persuaded that there are cases where justice can only be served by confining the parties to their rights under prenuptial agreements, we should be cautious about too categorically asserting the contrary.* I can find nothing in s.25 to compel a conclusion, so much at odds with personal freedoms to make arrangements for

---

14   [1995] 2 F.L.R. 45 at p.66. My italics.
15   [1997] 2 F.L.R. 100 at p.102.
16   Ibid., at p.103. My italics.

ourselves, that escape from solemn bargains, carefully struck by informed adults, is readily available here. It all depends.

The circumstances of the two cases were quite different. In *F v. F* the standard of provision for the wife under two pre-nuptial agreements was ridiculously low in the light of the fact that the husband was extremely wealthy. Although it was said that the agreements would have been strictly enforced in Germany, which was the country of origin of both parties, Thorpe J. declined to allow expert evidence of German law. He did not think that even in Germany the wife would not have the right to deploy a case either that there was some inequality of bargaining power, alternatively undue influence, or that they are inconsistent with social policy in Germany.[17] For the purposes of his determination he did not attach any significant weight to those contracts. In contrast in *S v. S* the pre-nuptial agreement executed in New York had been negotiated at length by professionals on behalf of worldly people. It made significant provision for the wife in the event of divorce and out of the husband's estate on his death. It was reached between parties who in the preceding three years had each suffered the distress of acrimonious divorce including in both cases the attempted invocation of rival jurisdictions. The wife conceded that she understood that the purpose of the pre-nuptial agreement was to obviate analogous distress in the event that the marriage failed. It was also agreed that the husband would not have entered into the marriage in the absence of the agreement. 'Thus, without the agreement, there would have been no marriage, no divorce and ... potential financial claims.'[18] It seems, therefore that had a stay not been granted, the pre-nuptial agreement would have been regarded as of considerable significance.

In the recent case of *M v. M (Prenuptial Agreement)*[19] a pre-nuptial agreement made by the parties in British Columbia which limited the wife's entitlement to the equivalent of £275,000 was clearly a significant factor even though it was not regarded as binding on the Court Connell J. said:[20]

> In my view it would be as unjust to the husband to ignore the existence of the agreement and its terms as it would be to the wife to hold her strictly to those terms. I do bear the agreement in mind as one of the more relevant circumstances of this case, but the court's overriding duty remains to attempt to arrive at a solution which is fair in all the circumstances, applying s.25 of the Matrimonial Causes Act 1973.

Moreover, even though a court is not bound by a pre-nuptial agreement and may attach little weight to its provisions in determining how to exercise its powers under the 1973 Act, where the agreement purports to determine the property rights of the spouses a court may recognise it as providing the basis for determining

---

17   [1995] 2 F.L.R. 45 at p.66.
18   [1997] 2 F.L.R. 100 at p.113.
19   [2002] 1 F.L.R. 654. Other relevant factors in departing from equality were the comparative shortness of the marriage (five years) and the fact that the husband had created the family wealth.
20   Ibid., at p.664, para.26.

whether any adjustment is appropriate under that Act. Thus in *Van den Boogaard v. Laumen*[21] the European Court of Justice was concerned with the question whether an order for payment of a lump sum or for the transfer of property under the 1973 Act was to be regarded as maintenance and so enforceable under the Brussels Convention. In making the orders in the original divorce proceedings Cazalet J. had said that he did not regard the separation of goods agreement made by the parties in the Netherlands as binding on him. The Advocate General said that it was clear from his judgment that he considered the agreement and its implications for the issues before him in some depth.[22]

> He appears in fact to have regarded it as applicable in so far as he assumed that the various matrimonial assets were owned separately by the former husband and wife in accordance with the agreement. He was not however prepared to find that the wife had abrogated any rights to further capital provision by virtue of the agreement.

The reasons which the judge gave for disregarding it to that extent appeared to be solely to do with the fairness of the agreement in the circumstances in which it was entered into.

Accordingly, in applications for financial provision under the 1973 Act, pre-nuptial agreements may be afforded some recognition in two ways. First, they may be recognised as establishing existing rights but as not preventing variation of those rights. Secondly, they may be recognised as affecting the way in which the court should exercise its jurisdiction to vary existing property rights. They are not, however, conclusive.

Application for a stay of divorce proceedings in England   In view of the differences between jurisdictions in relation to matrimonial property and maintenance it is not surprising that where divorce proceedings may be commenced in more than one jurisdiction, spouses will form different views as to the most advantageous forum for the resolution of their affairs. The wide discretionary powers of the court in England and Wales under the Matrimonial Causes Act 1973 to order not only financial provision, but also to adjust property rights, is likely to be attractive to a spouse faced with a divorce in a jurisdiction where the courts possess only limited powers in relation to property and financial provision on divorce. The other spouse may prefer a jurisdiction where the matrimonial property rights of the parties are predetermined whether by a statutory scheme or by a pre-nuptial agreement which will be recognised as binding. This may lead to a battle over the forum for the divorce proceedings with one or perhaps both spouses applying for a stay of proceedings in what they respectively perceive as the unattractive forum. In such circumstances an English court will look 'first to see what factors there are which connect the case with another forum. If, on the basis of that inquiry, the court concludes that there is another available forum which, prima facie, is clearly more appropriate for the trial of the action, it will

---

[21]   [1997] Q.B. 759.
[22]   Ibid., at p.778, para.71.

ordinarily grant a stay, unless there are circumstances by reason of which justice requires that a stay should nevertheless not be granted...'.[23]

In the course of such an application to the court in England, the existence of a pre-nuptial agreement made in the other forum may be an important factor in the court's decision whether or not to grant a stay. This was the case in *R v. R (Divorce: Stay of Proceedings)*[24] and in *S v. S (Divorce: Staying Proceedings)*[25] In the latter case the pre-nuptial agreement executed in New York in the circumstances described earlier and purporting to be governed by New York law was a significant factor in the decision to grant a stay of a petition in England. Wilson J., emphasising the need to balance fairness, said that he had been persuaded that New York was clearly more appropriate than England as a forum for the proceedings for divorce and for the determination of financial issues between the parties. This was so even though a stay of the English proceedings would make it unlikely that the wife would be able to claim any further financial provision beyond that provided for in the pre-nuptial agreement. In reaching that conclusion he had borne very much in mind the wife's primary residence in England, as well as her close past links with New York. He had also paid considerable regard to the husband's primary residence, established over many years, in New York. Nevertheless, he said:[26]

> ... the provisions of the prenuptial agreement, both the substantive financial provisions and in particular the provisions as to forum, have weighed heavily with me. *Even if (which I doubt) this agreement were to be of very limited significance in any substantive analysis by this court of the wife's financial claims pursuant to s.25 of the 1973 Act, it in no way follows that it must be of very limited significance in the despatch of the current application. Fairness requires otherwise.*

As from March 1, 2000 the position in relation to jurisdiction has changed as between Member States of the European Union. Under the Convention on Jurisdiction and the Recognition Enforcement of Judgments in Matrimonial Matters (Brussels II) the courts in the state in which proceedings are first commenced by one party will have jurisdiction in preference to the courts in which proceedings may subsequently be commenced by the other party.[27] The existence of a pre-nuptial contract may, however, continue to be a relevant factor in cases not coming within Brussels II.

Applications for financial provision after a foreign divorce   Where a marriage has been dissolved by a foreign decree, a court in England has no jurisdiction to order financial provision under the Matrimonial Causes Act 1973. In such circumstances a party to the dissolved marriage may seek financial provision by means of an application under Part III of the Matrimonial and Family Proceedings

---

23   See *de Dampierre v. de Dampierre* [1988] A.C. 92:
24   [1994] 2 F.L.R. 1036.
25   [1997] 2 F.L.R. 100.
26   Ibid., at p.114. My italics.
27   Article 11.

Act 1984. The existence of a pre-nuptial agreement may be an important factor in the decision of the court on whether or not to grant leave to make an application under the 1984 Act. This was the case in *N v. N*[28] where the parties were Swedish nationals who had entered into a pre-nuptial agreement in Sweden to the effect that neither of them would derive any benefit from the other consequent upon their divorce. It provided:

> All property which each of us has acquired or will acquire for and during the marriage through inheritance, testament, gift, own work or otherwise shall be the individual property of the person by whom it is acquired, with the other having no right to half of the property held by the other party to the marriage.

The parties were subsequently divorced, with the husband's consent, in Sweden, but no application for financial relief appeared to have been made by either party. The wife moved to London and the husband sought and obtained leave to apply for financial relief under the 1984 Act. Granting the wife's application to have the order for leave set aside. Cazalet J. considered that the failure of the husband to have various financial matters dealt with by the Swedish court would outweigh the other consideration arising under s.16 such that the court would not regard is as appropriate for an order to be made in the English court. He continued:[29]

> Furthermore the Swedish court, in my view, is the appropriate court in which to decide the effect of the prenuptial agreement. It would be binding in Sweden as against being no more than a material consideration in this court under s.25 of the Matrimonial Causes Act 1973. Indeed, by coming to this court the husband may obtain an advantage in that the court here in considering its award can step outside the constriction of the prenuptial agreement and may grant the husband more than his entitlement under Swedish law by taking into consideration the wife's overall assets, including her inheritance from her father, a matter expressly excluded from the husband's reach by the prenuptial agreement.

Agreements made in England and Wales

As indicated in the Introduction, agreements made in England have recently been considered by the courts exercising powers to order financial provision and property adjustment under the Matrimonial Causes Act 1973. *In K v. K (Ancillary Relief: Prenuptial Agreement)*[30] the agreement provided that in the event of the separation of the parties for six months or more, or the dissolution of the marriage within five calendar years of the date of the agreement, the husband would pay to the wife £100,000 to be increased by 10 per cent per annum compound. It was clear from this and from the negotiations preceding the agreement that the parties intended the agreement to have effect only in the event of a short marriage. The marriage did indeed prove to be short lived and on the wife's application for

28   [1997] 1 F.L.R. 900.
29   Ibid., at pp.912-913.
30   [2003] 1 F.L.R. 120 at p.132.

ancillary relief the pre-nuptial agreement proved to be decisive so far as capital was concerned though periodical payments were ordered in her favour.[31] Roger Hayward Smith Q.C. sitting as a High Court judge held that no injustice would be done to the wife by holding her to the agreement in respect of capital. Indeed it would be unjust to the husband if the agreement was ignored. He said:[32]

> This was a very short marriage. The wife contributed nothing to the husband's wealth. The husband married the wife only under pressure from her family and on the understanding that the wife's capital claim in the event of a short marriage would be governed by the agreement which both the husband and the wife and her family wanted.

Objections to pre-nuptial agreements

A threat to marriage?

In general terms, pre-nuptial agreements have traditionally been seen as not compatible with, and as denigrating the status of, marriage. They were seen as tending to facilitate divorce by providing inducements to end the marriage. Thus in *N v. N (Jurisdiction: Prenuptial Agreement)*[33] Wall J. said that ' ... an agreement made prior to marriage which contemplates the steps the parties will take in the event of divorce or separation is perceived as being contrary to public policy because it undermines the concept of marriage as a life-long union'. Moreover, marriage has been seen as a contract with set terms, and to permit undue modification of those terms would strike at the heart of marriage. This extends to matters of property and finance as Thorpe L.J. said in *F v. F (Ancillary Relief: Substantial Assets)* in the passage already quoted.[34] However, more recently, in *M v. M (Prenuptial Agreement)* Connell J. said:[35]

> The public policy objection to such agreements, namely that they tend to diminish the importance of the marriage contract, seems to me to be of less importance now that divorce is so commonplace.

Prenuptial agreements have also been criticised as a bad beginning for a marriage by focussing on material matters at a time when emotions suggest otherwise. In the United States it has been suggested that they introduce the grasping 'morals of the marketplace' into an intimate relationship and undermine the co-operative goals of marriage.[36]

However, even if marriage is confined to the traditional 'union for life of one

---

[31] The agreement made no provision for periodical payments for the wife.
[32] Ibid., at p.132.
[33] [1999] 2 F.L.R. 745 at p.752.
[34] [1995] 2 F.L.R. 45 at p.66. See text at footnote 13.
[35] [2002] 1 F.L.R. 654 at p.661, para.21.
[36] See Weitzman, *The Marriage Contract: Spouses Lovers and the Law* (1981) at p.243 where the arguments are considered, and Marston, *Planning for Love: The Politics of Prenuptial Agreements* (1997) 49 Stanford L.R. 887 at p.894.

man and one woman', it is in practice much more varied than is implied by the traditional view – as Weitzman in her leading work, *The Marriage, Contract, Spouses, Lovers and the Law*,[37] has shown. In particular, the assumption that it is the first marriage for both parties is not justified in an increasing number of cases. There may be children from previous marriages and the parties may no longer be young. Marriages are more varied than the traditional view implies so that the standards of financial provision that are 'intended to be of universal application' are difficult to apply. Indeed this variety is a justification for the wide discretionary powers now possessed by English courts on divorce. What this system does not provide is certainty, and certainty is an important consideration especially for older spouses with existing assets and responsibilities.

It has been argued that the negotiation of, and entry into, a pre-nuptial agreement may cause the parties to face up to potential sources of disagreement and may either 'save them from a disastrous marriage' or enhance their relationship once married by enabling them to discuss financial matters more easily after marriage. Facing up to questions about property and finance before marriage may prevent disagreements about such matters after marriage.[38] In the United States '[c]ourts have argued that prenuptial agreements might actually encourage marriage. If previously married individuals can't contract to avoid the most unpleasant aspects of divorce, they might simply choose not to get married'.[39] This point is echoed by the Government in their Consultation paper *Supporting Families* where it is stated that:[40]

> Providing greater security on property matters in this way could make it more likely that some people would marry, rather than simply live together. It might also give couples in a shaky marriage a little greater assurance about their future than they might otherwise have had.

On the other hand, the judges of the Family Division in their *Response to Government Proposals* on the reform of the law of ancillary relief, express reservations about whether the law should strive to encourage pre-nuptial agreements.[41] They state:

> We all still believe strongly in the institution of marriage as a source of personal and social stability and wonder whether the pre-nuptial agreement conditions the couple to the failure of their marriage and so helps to precipitate it.

---

37   Ibid.

38   See Marston, loc.cit. at pp.894-896 and the U.S. sources quoted there.

39   Marston, loc.cit. at p. 896 referring to *Brooks v. Brooks* 733 P. 2d 1044, 1050 (Alaska 1987) and *Gant v. Gant* 329 S.E. 2d 106, 113 (W.Va. 1985).

40   Para.4.22. In Australia Fehlberg and Smyth found that '[r]elationship tension reportedly increased when the parties and their legal representatives began formal negotiations regarding the terms of the agreement'. (2002) 16 I.J.L.P. & F. 127 at p.135. In some cases difficulties led not only to the abandonment of the agreement, but also of the relationship.

41   The Response was made by way of submission to the Lord Chancellor's Ancillary Relief Advisory Group and is set out in [1999] Family Law 159-163.

This is a question which they believe deserves research. Some judges also felt 'that the institution of marriage is devalued if, while entering it, a couple can elect to sever some of its most important, if contingent, legal effects. Other judges considered, 'hesitantly, that marriage is made for mankind, not vice versa, and that, subject to obvious limits, adults should be allowed to cast their relationships in their own way'. The majority of the judges were of the view that 'slightly, but only slightly, greater prominence might be given to the nuptial agreement [i.e. post as well as pre-nuptial] in the law of ancillary relief'. Specifically, the majority view was that 'an additional matter might be added into s.25(2), at (i), namely the terms of any agreement reached between the parties in contemplation of or subsequent to their marriage'. A minority would go a little further despite the 'unanimous lack of enthusiasm for the pre-nuptial agreement'. This would frame the provision in the form that a pre- or post-nuptial agreement would be enforced 'unless ...'.

The public interest

A pre-nuptial agreement, by limiting or excluding one spouse's claim on the assets, capital and income of the other spouse, might have the effect of leaving the former without adequate means of support. The result might be to force that spouse to depend on state support so that the state has a very practical and financial interest in ensuring that proper support is not excluded.[42]

The first point to be made in relation to this argument is that support is one thing, a share of capital assets is another. The two are, of course, linked in that the provision of capital resources reduces the need for income support, but the need to ensure adequate support is no justification for invalidating agreements limiting the right of, say, a second spouse to share in capital assets inherited from the other spouse's family or built up over a long first marriage the children of which would have been regarded by the deceased former spouse as having an important claim. The combination of support and property considerations in the 1973 Act has widened the search for assets to provide support, and 'there are no protected funds' even in estates of substantial size.[43] Secondly, the claim for support may not be a strong one in a second marriage late in life.

The public interest is also important in relation to a child of the family. Whether or not a child of the family was born at the time of the agreement, he or she will not be a party to the agreement and his or her rights cannot be eroded by the agreement. As the judges have pointed out in their *Response*, this is not merely a matter of preventing any restriction on the powers of the court to order provision for any such child. Thus if the entitlement of the parent with care of a child is restricted, for example, in relation to the home occupied by her, then the child may be prejudiced.[44]

---

[42]   This is reflected in the rule in *Hyman v. Hyman* [1929] A.C. 601 and s.34 of the Matrimonial Causes Act 1973.
[43]   *Pearce v. Pearce* [1980] 1 F.L.R. 261.
[44]   See [1999] Family Law 159 at p.162.

Abuse of dominant position

Another potential danger with a pre-nuptial agreement is that the parties may not have been in an equal bargaining position. There may have been unfair pressure on the weaker party – usually the wife – to enter into the agreement which will delimit the husband's future responsibilities. Clearly, there is a danger that the limitations imposed by a pre-nuptial agreement could operate unfairly on the termination of a marriage which has endured for many years – whether it is a first or subsequent marriage for one or both of the parties. It is important to ensure an appropriate standard of provision for a spouse on termination of a marriage. However, in the absence of undue pressure there can be advantages for the weaker party in being assured of a certain standard of provision. Indeed '[w]omen, who have traditionally had less power, may feel their rights are best protected if they are formalized'.[45] If there are strong reasons for a wealthy man with an existing family entering into a marriage late in life wishing to delimit his future financial obligations to protect his family, wealth and business from uncertainty on his death or divorce, a wife may be reassured by an agreement which removes uncertainty in a situation where the marriage may be much shorter and the fruits of the marriage partnership are likely to be much less than in a marriage to a younger man.[46] In any event it is not only men who have existing families and substantial wealth. A widow may have just as much need for the protection and certainty of an agreement as a widower.[47]

Changed circumstances

Where the circumstances of the parties change dramatically over the period of the marriage it may be thought to be unfair to hold the parties to an agreement based on totally different expectations. Such an objection is likely to be relevant

---

[45] See Weitzman, loc. cit., p.241 where she considers the reasons why she discovered that men are more likely than women to assert that marriage contracts destroy trust.

[46] See cases of later marriage such as *S v. S* [1977] Fam. 127 where expectations could be regarded as limited.

[47] In an article published before the new Australian legislation permitting pre-nuptial agreements came into force, Fehlberg and Smyth, drawing upon relevant overseas and Australian empirical research, thought that binding pre-nuptial agreements were likely to offer more to men than women in terms of increased control and choice over how property is divided on marriage breakdown because of women's weaker economic position. (*Prenuptial agreements for Australia: why not?* (2000) 14 Australian Jo. of Family Law 80) In their subsequent article looking at the operation of the new legislation after one year, they said that it did not appear 'on the very limited evidence available to date that men rather than women are seeking to enter pre-nuptial agreements'. This appeared to be in contrast to United States evidence that such agreements were particularly likely to work to disadvantage women. They said that perhaps 'this view requires qualification in relation to older women with property and financial resources who are entering second marriages'. (*Binding Pre-Nuptial Agreements in Australia: The First Year* (2002) 16 I.J.L.P.& F. 127 at p.134.)

principally when the parties were of limited means at the date of the agreement. If, say, the husband acquires considerable wealth through inheritance, is the position very different from that of the husband who had great wealth at the date of the marriage which he wished to safeguard? The position seems more difficult if his wealth has been acquired by success in business especially as the contribution of the wife in one way or another is likely to have been important. The length of the marriage and the respective contributions of the parties will be unknown. Indeed the extent of the property that will be available on the termination of a marriage may be uncertain. This seems a real concern, though it also seems unlikely that an agreement would have been entered into in these circumstances. A pre-nuptial agreement is most likely to be used where the position is clearer and the objective is likely to be to safeguard particular interests such as the family business and inherited property, especially where there are children from a previous marriage.

The form of recognition and safeguards

Safeguards

Although pre-nuptial agreements pose dangers and problems in some situations, there are circumstances in which there is, it is submitted, a strong case for affording greater recognition to pre-nuptial agreements. It is in these circumstances – where the parties may have married late in life, may have established families with a claim on family property, may have family wealth or businesses which it is sought to protect – that pre-nuptial agreements are more likely to be made. However, if greater recognition is to be given to such agreements then proper safeguards are clearly necessary. What form should recognition take and how should the safeguards be provided?

Prior approval by a court would not seem feasible or acceptable in relation to pre-nuptial agreements.[48] Mere recognition of the validity of pre-nuptial agreements made in England would not provide the desired degree of certainty if they were merely a factor to be taken into account by the court in exercising discretion. This would place them in the same position as post-separation agreements and subject to the criticisms made by Hoffman L.J. in *Pounds v. Pounds.*[49] To achieve a degree of certainty an agreement needs to be binding subject to appropriate safeguards.

The safeguards must certainly be concerned with the circumstances in which the agreement was made so as to ensure what has been called procedural fairness. Procedural or formal fairness is concerned with the process by which the agreement was reached as distinct from the substance of the agreement. Should there also be safeguards to ensure substantive fairness, that is, to ensure fairness of the bargain? Safeguards surrounding the formation of an agreement, by reducing

---

48   This is the position in relation to exclusion of claims by a spouse under the Inheritance (Provision for Family and Dependants) Act 1975 though this can only occur on the grant of a decree of divorce, nullity or judicial separation.

49   [1994] 1 F.L.R. 775 at p.791.

pressure and increasing information and reflection, are likely to have some impact on the contents of an agreement and may go some way to preventing unfairness. However, should a court be given power to review the substantive fairness of an agreement following termination of the marriage by divorce or death? If such a power of review is too wide and is exercised too frequently, then advantages of pre-nuptial agreements would be much reduced and the position much the same as now exists.

Experience from other jurisdictions

In determining safeguards there is overseas experience upon which to draw. In New Zealand, the Property (Relationships) Act, formerly the Matrimonial Property Act 1976,[50] provides that any two persons in contemplation of their marriage to each other may, for the purpose of contracting out of the provisions of that Act, make such agreement with respect to the status, ownership and division of their property (including future property) as they think fit. This is subject to a number of procedural safeguards and such an agreement will also be set aside if the court is satisfied that it would be unjust to give effect to it.

In Ontario the Family Law Act 1986,[51] provides that 'A man and a woman who are married to each other or intend to marry may enter into an agreement in which they agree on their respective rights and obligations under the marriage or on separation, on the annulment or dissolution of the marriage or on death, including (a) ownership in or division of property; (b) support obligations; (c) the right to direct the education and moral training of their children, but not the right to custody of or access to their children; and (d) any other matter in the settlement of their affairs'. Subsection (2) provides that a provision in a marriage contract purporting to limit a spouse's rights under Part II (Matrimonial Home) is unenforceable.

In Australia the Family Law Act 1975[52] provides that people who are contemplating entering into a marriage with each other may make a written agreement regarding the way in which, in the event of the breakdown of the marriage, all or any of the property or financial resources of either or both of them at the time when the agreement is made, or at a later time and before the dissolution of the marriage, is to be dealt with, or as to the maintenance of either of them. Such a 'financial agreement' will be binding on the parties if certain conditions are satisfied.[53] A court may make an order setting aside a financial agreement in certain specified circumstances.[54]

In the United States the Uniform Premarital Act enables the parties to a prospective marriage to enter into a 'premarital agreement' dealing, *inter alia*, with

---

[50]   s.21. The Act also now applies to any two persons in contemplation of entering into a *de facto* relationship and to spouses and *de facto* partners.
[51]   s.52(1).
[52]   Part VIII of the Family Law Act 1975, s.90B inserted by the Family Law Amendment Act 2000.
[53]   s.90G.
[54]   s.90K.

'the rights and obligations of each of the parties in any of the property of either or both of them whenever and wherever acquired or located', 'the disposition of property upon separation, marital dissolution, death or the occurrence or non-occurrence of any event', and 'the modification or elimination of support'.[55] There are a number of procedural safeguards and a premarital agreement is not enforceable if the party against whom enforcement is sought proves that, *inter alia*, the agreement was unconscionable when it was executed and, before execution of the agreement, that party was not provided with a fair and reasonable disclosure of the property or financial obligations of the other party.[56]

Government proposals

In the Consultation Paper *Supporting Families* the Government proposed to protect the interests of a party to the agreement who is economically weaker and the interests of children through six safeguards.[57] If one or more of the six specified circumstances was found to apply the written agreement would not be legally binding. Three of these safeguards are clearly concerned with procedural fairness and three are directed in varying degrees to substantive content of the agreement.

Procedural safeguards

Formalities and independent legal advice   The first avoiding ground suggested in the *Proposals* is where one or both of the couple did not receive independent legal advice before entering into the agreement. The New Zealand Act also requires each party to have had independent legal advice and every agreement must be in writing signed by both parties. The signature of each party must be witnessed by a lawyer, and the witness must certify that before the party whose signature he has witnessed signed the agreement he has explained to that party the effect and implications of the agreement.[58]

The Australian legislation also requires each party to have received independent legal advice in relation to certain specific matters before entering into the written agreement which must be signed by both parties. The agreement must also contain a statement that each party has received such and the annexure to the agreement must contain a certificate signed by the person providing the independent legal advice stating that the advice was provided.[59]

The Ontario Family Law Reform Act provides that a marriage contract is unenforceable if it is not 'in writing, signed by the parties and witnessed'.[60] The need for disclosure is emphasised by s.56(2)(a). Independent legal advice is not

---

[55]   s.3. The Uniform Premarital Agreement Act, s.1 defines a premarital agreement as an agreement between prospective spouses made in contemplation of marriage and to be effective on marriage.

[56]   s.6.

[57]   Home Office (1998), para.4.23.

[58]   s.21F of the amended Act.

[59]   s.90G.

[60]   s.55.

expressly required but an agreement can be set aside if either party does not 'understand the nature [or] consequences' of the agreement.

The Uniform Premarital Agreement Act also requires an agreement to be in writing and it must be signed by both parties. An agreement is not enforceable if the party against whom enforcement is sought proves that he or she did not execute the agreement voluntarily. Independent legal advice is not specifically required but the Commentary states that nothing in the provision makes the absence of the assistance of independent legal counsel a condition for the unenforceability of an agreement. However, lack of that assistance may well be a factor in determining whether the conditions for enforceability may have existed.[61]

Disclosure   The second ground for invalidity is where one or both of the couple have failed to give full disclosure of assets and property before the agreement was made. This is not specifically mentioned in the New Zealand Act, but it will clearly be relevant when the court considers substantive unfairness. Under the Australian legislation, it is specifically provided that the independent legal advice must cover, *inter alia*, (i) the effect of the agreement on the rights of a party; (ii) whether or not at the time when the advice provided, it was to the advantage, financially or otherwise, of that party to make the agreement; and (iii) whether or not, at that time, it was prudent for that party to make the agreement.[62] Such advice can only properly be given if there has been a proper disclosure and an agreement may be set aside if it was obtained by fraud 'including non-disclosure of a material matter'.[63]

The Uniform Premarital Agreement Act provides that an agreement is not enforceable if the party against whom enforcement is sought proves that '(2) the agreement was unconscionable when it was executed and, before execution of the agreement, that party (i) was not provided a fair and reasonable disclosure of the property or financial obligations of the other party; (ii) did not voluntarily and expressly waive, in writing, such disclosure or further disclosure, and (iii) did not have, or reasonably could not have had, an adequate knowledge of the property or financial obligations of the other party'.[64]

Time of execution   The third proposed ground for invalidity is where the agreement is made fewer than 21 days prior to the marriage This would prevent a nuptial agreement being forced on people shortly before their wedding day, when they may not feel able to resist. A similar requirement does not feature in either the New Zealand or Australian legislation or in the Uniform U.S. Act. However, the effect of execution close to the marriage had been considered by a New Zealand court. In *Wood v. Wood*[65] the husband told the wife on the day before their wedding that he would not proceed with the marriage unless the wife signed an agreement excluding the operation of the general principle of equal sharing in the

---

[61]   See e.g. *Del Vecchio v. Del Vecchio* 43 So. 2d 17 (Fla. 1962).
[62]   s.90G.
[63]   s.90K.
[64]   Para.6(a).
[65]   [1998] 3 N.Z.L.R. 234.

1976 Act. Fisher J. could see no justification for interfering with the judge's finding that it was the pressure of the impending wedding which finally motivated the wife to return to her solicitor and sign the agreement. However, whether this was a situation of the husband's making was another matter. It was clear that for a substantial period – probably about three months – she had known that the husband wanted a pre-nuptial agreement and she had given every appearance of negotiating the exact form of the agreement over the final three weeks or so. Fisher J. said: 'It could not have been a cause for surprise that the husband would want it to be signed before the wedding rather than after it. Once the wedding was over he would lose his bargaining power. The statutory regime would also begin to affect the very assets he was trying to protect. All the drafts and copies of the agreement were expressed as pre-nuptial agreements, not post-nuptial ones. It cannot have escaped the notice of the wife and her solicitor that the form of this agreement presupposed that it would be signed before the wedding.'[66] He concluded that the wife had allowed a situation to develop in which, knowing that the husband would require an agreement as a precondition for marriage, she continued with preparations for the wedding. The fact that matters had to be rushed at the last minute could not logically be laid at the door of the husband. A rigid time limit may therefore be thought inappropriate.

In two recent English cases a pre-nuptial agreement had been signed shortly before the marriage. In *M v. M (Prenuptial Agreement)* Connell J. noted that the objectives of the parties were somewhat different. He said:[67]

> The husband was determined to limit the financial consequences of the marriage which the wife required if she was to give birth to their child. The wife could not contemplate giving birth without being married; and was unwilling to contemplate the possibility of cancelling a wedding for which invitations had been sent to many guests ...

Nevertheless, even though the agreement had been signed by the parties shortly before their marriage, Connell J. found that the wife did have the opportunity of seeking independent legal advice though she chose not to follow it and signed the agreement.

In *K v. K (Ancillary Relief: Prenuptial Agreement)*[68] the wife had signed the pre-nuptial agreement three days before the marriage. Roger Hayward Smith Q.C. sitting as High Court judge found that the wife had understood the agreement and was properly advised as to its terms. The husband had not put pressure on her to sign the agreement and the judge did not accept that she felt under any other pressure at the time she signed it. She willingly signed the agreement and the husband had not exploited a dominant position.

General contractual principles   It is also proposed that an agreement would not be legally binding '... where under the general law of contract the agreement is

66   Ibid., at p.239.
67   [2002] 1 F.L.R. 654 at p.656, para.6.
68   [2003] 1 F.L.R. 120 at p.131.

unenforceable, including if the contract attempted to lay an obligation on a third party who had not agreed in advance'.[69] This would seem also to be concerned with traditional grounds on which a contract may be attacked, mistake, misrepresentation, duress and unconscionability. While concerned with formal fairness it does also touch on the merits of the bargain. Fraud and unconscionability are specifically mentioned in the Australian legislation as grounds for setting aside an agreement.[70]

The substantive provisions of an agreement

Fairness   An agreement would also not be binding '... where the court considers that the enforcement of the agreement would cause significant injustice to one or both of the couple or a child of the marriage'.[71] This clearly raises the substantive fairness of the agreement as an issue.

It has been noted that the New Zealand Act provides that an agreement may be set aside if the court is satisfied that it would be unjust to give effect to it. In deciding whether it would unjust to give effect to an agreement the court is required to take into account:[72]

(a) the provisions of the agreement;
(b) the length of time that has elapsed since the agreement was entered into;
(c) whether the agreement was unfair or unreasonable in the light of all the circumstances at the time it was entered into;
(d) whether the agreement has become unfair or unreasonable in the light of any changes in circumstances since it was entered into (whether or not those changes were foreseen by the parties);
(e) any other matters that the Court considers relevant.

Under the Australian legislation the independent legal advice must specifically deal with 'whether or not, at the time of the advice and in the light of such circumstances as were, at that time, reasonably foreseeable, the provisions of the agreement were fair and reasonable'.[73] Moreover, amongst the grounds on which an agreement may be set aside is the fact that 'in the circumstances that have arisen since the agreement was made it is impracticable for the agreement or a part of the agreement to be carried out'.[74]

In looking at substantive fairness there are two essential factors. The first is the background or expectations against which the fairness of the agreement is to be judged. This comprises not only the factual background, but also the legal background. In *Wood v. Wood* Fisher J. said in relation to s.21 of the New Zealand

---

69	*Supporting Families*, para.4.23.
70	s.90K.
71	Supporting Families, para.4.23.
72	s.21(10).
73	Family Law Act 1975, s.90G.
74	s.90K.

Family Property Act that 'it is usually difficult to decide whether it would be unjust to give effect to an agreement without considering the alternative result under the Act'.[75] That provision is in an Act which provides for equal sharing subject to certain qualifications. Fisher J. noted that the protection of pre-marriage assets, third-party gifts and inheritances had always been seen as one of the principal legitimate objects of contracting out.[76] He said: 'Attempts to contract out of the equal sharing of property acquired during the marriage (other than third party-gifts and inheritances) would therefore seem an uphill battle.'[77] On the other hand, it would 'be difficult to successfully challenge as unreasonable an agreement which, on its proper interpretation, does no more than to protect existing separate property, preserving the statutory regime for future acquired matrimonial property ....'[78] When made against the background of a discretionary system it would seem more difficult to judge its reasonableness – but it is a factor in the test for post-separation agreements set out in *Edgar v. Edgar*.[79]

The second factor is the effect of changes in the circumstances of the parties between the execution of the agreement and the termination of the marriage when one party seeks to enforce the agreement. A substantial period of time may elapse between those events. The wealth of one or both of the parties may have greatly increased, children may have been born, the health of one of the parties may have deteriorated as may earning capacity. Is the fairness of the agreement to be judged on the basis of the circumstances as they existed at the time the agreement was executed or at the time when it comes to be enforced? A review on the basis of fairness judged in the light of circumstances at the time of enforcement reduces the certainty and predictability which such an agreement seeks to achieve and the interest of a spouse who married in reliance on the agreement may be unfairly prejudiced.

The approach adopted in some United States jurisdictions has been to distinguish between agreements affecting property distribution and agreements affecting support obligations. The former should be assessed in the light of the circumstances as they existed at the time of execution, while the latter need to be assessed in the light of circumstances at the time of divorce.[80] This is apparently on the basis that the State has a greater interest in ensuring adequate support than in the division of property and that this justifies greater supervision of such agreements. The difficulty with this approach is that the amount of support

---

75   [1998] 3 N.Z.L.R. 234 at p.239.

76   As illustrated by *Lowry v. Lowry* [1994] N.Z.F.L.R. 529.

77   Per Fisher J. in *Wood v. Wood* [1998] 3 N.Z.L.R. 234 at pp.241-242.

78   Ibid., at p.242.

79   [1980] 1 W.L.R. 1410.

80   Atwood, *Ten Years Later: Lingering Concerns About the Uniform Premarital Agreement Act* (1993) 19 Jo. of Legislation 127 at pp.139-140. If the effect of the modification or elimination of support causes a party to become eligible for support under a programme of public assistance the other party may be required to provide support notwithstanding the terms of the agreement: para.6(b). See also s.90F of the Family Law Act 1975 in Australia.

necessary for a spouse with no independent earning capacity will depend to a great extent on the amount of property which that spouse has following termination of the marriage. For couples with modest means the distinction may be difficult, if not impossible, to draw particularly as in England and Wales the distinction between the division of property and the provision of support has not been so clearly drawn in the legislation as in other jurisdictions. However, pre-nuptial agreements are probably much less likely to be encountered in such cases than in cases where one party has brought substantial assets into the marriage or acquired them by gift or inheritance during the marriage. In the latter situation the other party's need for support is likely to be much more easily distinguished from the division of property.

Another approach, suggested by Professor Oldham, is to make an agreement unenforceable only if the circumstances at the time of the termination of the marriage were substantially different from those which existed at the time of the execution of the agreement and such circumstances were not foreseeable at that time.[81] Thus he suggests that it would not be an unforeseeable change of circumstance if a spouse merely increases his or her earning capacity during marriage, but if a spouse developed health problems during marriage this would justify review of the agreement. 'On this approach an agreement would not become unenforceable merely because it was unfair at the time of divorce or because it was unwise...' More difficult is 'whether the ramifications of having a child are unforeseeable'. This suggestion may be contrasted with the New Zealand provision which refers to changes in circumstances 'whether or not those changes were foreseen by the parties'.

The existence/birth of a child of the family   One change which is likely to be of great significance is the birth of a child of the parties. Such an event may have been unforeseeable and is almost certain to involve a substantial change in the circumstances of the parties.[82] However, it may be unsatisfactory to leave such an event to be dealt with on this basis. Apart from any dispute about whether it was foreseen, it may be argued that even if it was foreseen review of the agreement is justified in the interests the child who was not a party to the agreement. The same is probably true where there is a child of the parties at the time of the agreement or a child who is or becomes a child of the family. The effect on an agreement of the birth or existence of a child seems best dealt with by a specific provision. The Government proposes that an agreement would not be legally enforceable '... where there is a child of the family, whether or not that child was alive or a child of the family at the time the agreement was made'.[83] The judges of the Family Division have expressed the view that 'the presence of a child should deprive the nuptial agreement of much if not all of its effect...' so that the role of the agreement

---

[81]   *Premarital Contracts are now Enforceable, Unless ...* (1984) 21 Houston L.R. 757 at p.778.

[82]   See Oldham, loc. cit. at p.779.

[83]   *Supporting Families*, para.4.23.

in the law would thereby be much circumscribed.[84]

Clearly the financial position of the child should not be prejudiced by a pre-nuptial agreement in the event of a divorce of the parents. Moreover, care of the child while dependent will have implications for the financial arrangements between the parents. This is specifically recognised in the Australian legislation. Amongst the grounds on which an agreement may be set aside is that 'since the making of the agreement, a material change in circumstances has occurred (being circumstances relating to the care, welfare and development of a child of the marriage) and as a result of the change, the child or, if the applicant has caring responsibility for the child ... a party to the agreement will suffer hardship if the court does not set the agreement aside'.[85] On the other hand, is it appropriate that the whole agreement should automatically be rendered unenforceable? One of the objectives of the agreement may have been the protection of the children of an earlier marriage, whose interests may otherwise receive little attention at the time of a second marriage – or a second divorce.

Conclusion

Pre-nuptial agreements can provide certainty and the means of protecting property which is not derived from the marriage partnership, such as pre-marriage assets, third-party gifts and inheritances, and existing family commitments such as children from a previous marriage. Such aspirations are not unreasonable though some may feel that this is subject to the proviso that the agreement does not unreasonably prevent an adequate level of support where this proves necessary. A pre-nuptial agreement may, however, cast its net more widely so as to encompass property to the acquisition of which both spouses may be regarded as making a contribution albeit in quite different ways. There is a difference between a family business of one party at the time of the agreement and a business largely built up during a marriage. This may point to the advantages of a discretionary system able to mould an answer to the particular circumstances of a case, but this would be at the price of certainty. The desired degree of certainty is not achieved merely by recognising the validity of a prenuptial agreement if it is no more than a factor to be taken into account by the court in the exercise of discretion.

Pre-nuptial agreements are unlikely to have a universal appeal, but this is no reason for not permitting such agreements for use in those cases where a desire for certainty in the light of existing assets and responsibilities is not unreasonable. In the *Response* of the Judges of the Family Division to *Government Proposals* the minority said:[86]

---

[84] *Response of the Judges of the Family Division to Government Proposals* [1999] Family Law 159. The majority were 'of the view that slightly, but only slightly, greater prominence might be given to the nuptial agreement in the law of ancillary relief'.

[85] Family Law Act 1975, s.90K(1)(d).

[86] *Response of the Judges of the Family Division* [1999] Family Law 159 at p.162.

The minority feels that the current law of ancillary relief has inherited a paternalistic strain, rather too hostile to contract (formerly collusion) and in this respect rather too jealous of its own discretion, for the protection, in effect of the downtrodden wife, and that, while she still exists, she may no longer be apt as a governing stereotype; ...

The objective should be an appropriate balance between certainty and fairness.[87] Legislation in other jurisdictions illustrates the ways in which such a balance may be sought by emphasising the importance of whether the agreement was entered into fairly and whether it represents a fair bargain. This is not to ignore the difficulties that that involves particularly as any power which the court is given to review the substantive fairness of an agreement and the exercise of that power must not be such as to destroy the certainty which is a vital objective of a pre-nuptial agreement.[88]

---

[87]   See Oldham, *Premarital Contracts are Now Enforceable, Unless* ... (1984) 21 Houston L.R. 757 at p.777.

[88]   See the comment of Wood J. in *Fisher v. Fisher* [1998] 3 N.Z.L.R. 234 at p.235.

Index